ECONAMERICA

Why the American Economy Is Alive and Well . . . And What that Means to Your Wallet

JEFF THREDGOLD

John Wiley & Sons, Inc.

Published by John Wiley & Sons, Inc., Hoboken, New Jersey.
Published simultaneously in Canada.

Wiley Bicentennial Logo: Richard J. Pacifico
Chapter opening image courtesy of Photodisc, Inc.

For general information on our other products and services or for technical support, please contact our Customer Care Department within the United States at (800) 762-2974, outside the United States at (317) 572-3993 or fax (317) 572-4002.

Wiley also publishes its books in a variety of electronic formats. Some content that appears in print may not be available in electronic books. For more information about Wiley products, visit our web site at www.wiley.com.

Library of Congress Cataloging-in-Publication Data:

Thredgold, Jeff, 1951-
    EconAmerica : why the American economy is alive and well . . . and what that means to your wallet / Jeff Thredgold.
        p.cm.
    Includes index.
    ISBN 978-0-470-09698-7 (cloth)
        1. United States—Economic conditions—2001-   I. Title.   II. Title: EconAmerica.
    HC106.83.T47 2007
    330.973—dc22   2007007056

Printed in the United States of America.

10 9 8 7 6 5 4 3 2 1

Contents

Preface

I learned a long time ago that I cannot have a useful discussion about "the economy" with a purely academic economist. To these university economists, almost everything fits into a mathematical equation. In the real world, it does not.

Consumer attitudes and human emotion are as powerful as any other forces impacting the world in which we live. Economics is simply "the study of life" and the choices we make.

Economics—also known as "the dismal science"—gets a bad rap too frequently as being vague and unscientific. To quote a friend, economics should get the respect it deserves alongside the other *occult* sciences.

Every decision people make is an economic decision. Critical choices about education, employment, earnings, and investing can contribute to a successful career and stress-free retirement, as opposed to a working life and retirement based on pinching pennies.

The American economy has performed well in recent years despite the painful shocks of global terrorism, sky-high energy prices, rising short-term interest rates, and volatile housing markets. Even as solid growth has occurred, the national media has led millions of Americans to believe that the economy is merely limping along, creating few quality jobs, and on the brink of disaster.

Such negativity dominates the economic writing found in the nation's bookstores. Books focusing on the demise of America; the coming debt crisis; the coming oil crisis; and the imminent dominance of China, Europe, or India are far too prevalent.

I served many years as chief economist of one of the nation's largest financial services firms and now enjoy a thriving business as a professional speaker and economic consultant. I have also been writing a weekly economic and financial newsletter for the past 32 years. Whether in writing or speaking, I have always tried to present a *balanced and optimistic* view of the global economy and America's role within it.

This country has a bright future. The American people have a bright future. This book, *econAmerica,* reflects my view of the way things are—including the good news and the bad news—and the way I think they should be.

econAmerica includes discussions of many critical areas within the U.S. economy, including government and taxation, the entitlement issue, the Federal Reserve, education, immigration, "bridging" to retirement, the stock market, currencies, global competitors, and the power of incentives in the economy.

This book can be of value to both novice and seasoned practitioners of economic study. It focuses on four key factors, or Silver Bullets, that combine to create a strong American economy in coming years.

Opportunities abound as much as ever before. An extremely tight U.S. labor market in coming years will lead to enhanced employee compensation and benefit programs offered by those companies that wish to keep their best and brightest on the job for years to come. In addition, I expect the stock market to perform well.

Today's opportunities for our young people are no less exciting than they were a generation ago. The Internet provides the means for small players to compete with the giants.

America's leadership role in the world will continue. Such leadership will occur despite the challenges from China, India, Japan, and a more cohesive Europe.

An important area of my work is forecasting the future. Forecasting is not easy—economists are wrong more often than we are right, for which we receive considerable and well-deserved abuse.

Economists give forecasts of the future *not* because we know what is going to happen. We give forecasts because we are *asked* to.

Forecasting is a major challenge because the economy is a moving target subject to whipsaw by unexpected events, which you can expect to occur just *after* you put a forecast (or a book) into print. For the latest on the economy, please sign up for the *Tea Leaf,* our free weekly economic and financial newsletter delivered via e-mail. Just visit www.thredgold.com.

I and many other economists will continue to provide forecasts for tomorrow. *Tea Leaf* readers and members of audiences I address yearly around the world will continue to challenge me, criticize me, and sometimes even agree with me.

In the meantime, I will continue to do what I love doing, that is, a combination of extensive writing and traveling in excess of 100,000 miles annually speaking *optimistically* about the future of America...

Acknowledgments

My deepest appreciation and sincere thanks go out to our team at the TEA Company, Thredgold Economic Associates, and especially to Kendall Oliphant, who has been with me since 2002. You have the enthusiasm and talent for what we can accomplish as a professional team. Your skills in problem solving, web development, layout, editing, computer systems, and most importantly seeing the big picture, are simply amazing. I hope to keep you on the team for years to come.

I want to thank my son, Shawn Thredgold, who joined us in 2004. Your efforts in marketing and supporting me as a professional speaker and economist are tremendous. Meeting planners frequently comment about your professionalism. Your attitude is always tops, and I truly enjoy working with you.

Ross E. Kendell deserves my gratitude as well—for hiring a wet-nosed kid to be a banker in 1973. My thanks also go to Richard K. Hemingway and Robert H. Bischoff, who guided my growth as an investment portfolio manager and later, after sending me to graduate school, as an economist.

I sincerely thank Victor J. Riley Jr., retired CEO of the $95 billion banking giant KeyCorp. In 1988, you saw in me raw talent as an economist and a speaker. You allowed me to serve as KeyCorp's Senior Vice President and Chief Economist from 1989 until 1994, and as Senior Vice President and Chief Business Economist for two more years, following the merger with Society Bancorporation. We did roughly 500 "dog-and-pony" shows (customer-oriented presentations at breakfast, lunch, and dinner) together from Maine to Alaska during those years. Because of your influence, I am now an active professional speaker.

I am indebted to Harris H. Simmons, A. Scott Anderson, and W. David Hemingway of the $47 billion Zions Bancorporation, Zions Bank, and Zions Bank Capital Markets, who allowed me to serve them and various Zions affiliate banks as economic consultant since 1997. I sincerely thank Robert L. Fenstermacher and Frank H. Hoell III of LibertyBank in Oregon, who provided me with a similar opportunity since 2003.

My gratitude is also extended to Audrey Gersh Lewis, Curtis Kelstrom, Robert and Sharron Horsey, and Earl and Donita Xaiz for their advice and friendship over the years—and to Debra W. Englander, Executive Editor at John Wiley & Sons. Thank you for seeing the value in how I think and communicate.

I would like to thank my parents Kevin and Donna Thredgold for always being there for me; my teenage daughters Kacey and Taylor for keeping me young; my adult children and their spouses, namely Amy and Drew, Christopher and Keri, Shawn and Tegan, and Michelle and Brett—and my nine grandchildren so far for reminding me how ancient I really am. Lastly, I wish to thank my wife Lynnette, known to me as LD, for the support and love you have honored me with for more than 20 years. You remain, as always, the most beautiful and multitalented woman I have ever known.

—Jeff Thredgold

CHAPTER 1

—THE ECONOMY—

U.S. ECONOMIC GROWTH

American economic performance has been quite impressive in recent years. What makes this newsworthy are the recent "shocks" to the economy including a mild recession in 2000 and 2001, the events of September 11, 2001, an extended period of interest rate hikes by the Federal Reserve, a near quadrupling of oil prices during the past few years, and the fits and starts of the nation's housing market.

U.S. economic growth over the past 25 years has occurred with only a modest period of economic decline. The two mildest recessions during the post–World War II period were of short duration in 1990 to 1991 and in 2000 to 2001. Aside from these modest economic contractions, the American economy grew at a pace ranging from subdued to robust for the majority of the 1981 to 2007 period.

Such an extended period of U.S. economic growth is a major departure from the more severe economic gyrations that characterized much of the nineteenth and twentieth centuries. Economic downturns in prior periods were typically more severe, with extended periods of economic decline "highlighted" by the Great Depression of 1929 to 1933. In fact, similar sharp declines of the American economy were almost commonplace in near 20-year cycles during the nineteenth century.

What accounts for this moderation in economic volatility? The most likely answers include more timely and accurate economic data as well as the enhanced ability of this nation's central bank, the Federal Reserve, to use monetary policy to smooth out economic volatility during the past 25 years.

The Past Dozen Years

Democrats are fond of boasting about the powerful U.S. economic growth that occurred during President Bill Clinton's second term

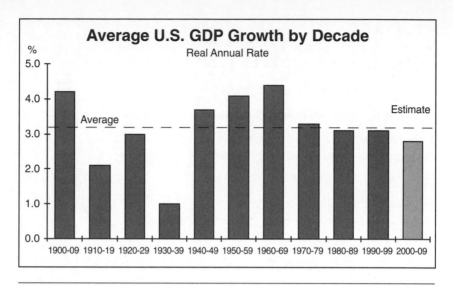

FIGURE 1.1   Average U.S. GDP

Source: Based on data from the U.S. Bureau of Economic Analysis.

from 1997 through 2000. Republicans are equally willing to boast of the solid economic performance of the 2003 to 2006 period, even as the national media tells a different story.

In fact, U.S. economic growth in both decades was merely in line with the average growth rate during the twentieth century, although performance of the global economy during these periods was very different. U.S. economic growth during the late 1990s was impressive given the fact that roughly half of the global economy had fallen into recession during 1998 and 1999. In contrast, U.S. economic growth of recent years was in tandem with solid economic performance around the world. (See Figure 1.1.)

Growth by Decade

Recent U.S. Economic Performance

The American economy has grown at a solid pace during the past four years. Many economists have referred to "the best of all worlds" mix of solid and extended U.S. economic growth, near-full employment, minimal inflation, and relatively low short- and long-term interest rates.

This growth has occurred even as the U.S. economy has faced two powerful headwinds that would have brought the economy to its knees during prior expansions. The first of these was extensive monetary tightening by the Federal Reserve. The Federal Reserve raised its key short-term interest rate 17 times between June 2004 and June 2006. In contrast, various prior periods of extensive monetary tightening to ward off inflation pressures soon found the U.S. economy flat on its back.

The second headwind was a painful spike in energy costs. Oil prices ranged from the mid-$20s to the mid-$70s during the past four years. Even so, U.S. economic growth continued at a solid pace. Such performance was a strong testament to the underlying strength and diversity of the American economy.

Solid global economic performance has also occurred, with the 2003 to 2006 period being the strongest four-year period since the early 1970s. Tens of millions of people around the world have seen their standards of living improve, even as the global community has experienced as much change as at any time in history.

The Late 1990s

Solid U.S. economic growth during much of the current decade compares to strong U.S. economic performance during the second half of the 1990s. Economic growth then was, in part, tied to the enormous expansion of the Internet and the surge in technology and other stocks. Unfortunately, the excesses of stock price appreciation resulted in a serious stock market meltdown in following years, contributing to the economic weakness that soon followed.

Another factor, in my opinion, that contributed to solid U.S. economic growth during the 1990s was split government. Democrats lost control of both the U.S. Senate and the U.S. House of Representatives in November 1994. The resulting Republican control of the Congress, combined with Democratic control of the White House, created an impasse regarding new policy. With only limited government interference, the American economy was allowed to work its own magic.

Split government, in my view, is at times the best government of all. This political reality of "don't do something, just stand there" was just what financial markets desired in the mid- to late 1990s. The result? Financial markets responded favorably, with powerful gains in stock prices in the years that followed.

Leadership

The U.S. role of dominance in the global economy during the past decade has been as clear-cut as at any time since the 1950s. As economists, we try to identify the critical industries of the future. I would currently identify seven:

- Technology
- Telecommunications
- Transportation
- Financial Services
- Energy
- Entertainment
- Bio-medicine

All seven of these industries currently find the United States as the principal player.

The Next Recession?

A question I am frequently asked when I give presentations to clients around the world is, "What could trigger the next U.S. recession?" Terrorism on American soil, avian flu, a major stock market plunge, and a general loss of confidence in the effectiveness of government typically come to mind.

In addition, the "headwinds" of sharply higher short-term interest rates and much higher energy prices could derail the expansion. More recently, economic pain associated with declining real estate values in various coastal markets and in the nation's Southwest could also contribute to renewed economic weakness.

GOODS AND SERVICES

The national media has consistently told a story of demise in recent years regarding America's ability "to make things." The common wisdom clearly states that this country has seen our manufacturing base move to Mexico and China.

As the story continues, millions of formerly high-paying goods production jobs have been replaced with jobs at fast-food restaurants. The common wisdom? We don't build or manufacture much anymore, we simply serve each other hamburgers and trade information with each other.

The common wisdom is largely misguided. American GDP (gross domestic product) is the total value of all goods produced and services provided in the economy. This total now exceeds $13.5 trillion annually.

We have not lost our ability to make things. We produce, manufacture, mine, and build more than ever before. We simply do it more efficiently than ever before.

Productivity Gains

According to the U.S. Bureau of Labor Statistics, we have lost a significant share of former manufacturing jobs. One of every six manufacturing jobs that existed in the United States seven years ago is gone. Thousands of jobs have been lost to lower-cost production facilities in Mexico, China, and other countries.

However, most of the decline in American manufacturing jobs has resulted directly from powerful gains in worker productivity. Manufacturing sector productivity gains have outpaced such gains in all other employment sectors in recent years.

We simply build products more efficiently than ever before. Given powerful technology and the use of more effective tools, it takes fewer people to produce a tire, fewer people to build a house, fewer people to strip-mine coal, and fewer people to operate most factories.

A good analogy notes that a hundred years ago roughly 50 percent of the American workforce was involved in agricultural production. Less than 3 percent of the workforce is involved in agricultural production today, with that share of workers producing a great deal more than ever before.

Higher Living Standards

Rising worker productivity is a key contributor to higher standards of living for American workers. From 1973 to 1995, U.S. productivity recorded lackluster average gains of just over 1 percent annually. Since then, productivity gains have grown at a much faster rate.

Average worker productivity rose at an average annual rate of 3.0 percent between 2002 and 2006, the strongest five-year period of gains in more than 40 years. It is likely, however, that productivity gains will slow somewhat as the current U.S. economic expansion becomes more mature. Is the economy long in the beard? In March 2007, the current U.S. economic expansion was 65 months in duration.

THE MISERY INDEX

One of the major political issues that greatly impacted results of U.S. presidential elections during 1976 and 1980 was frequent reference to "the misery index." This so-called "index" was simply the sum of the nation's most recent unemployment rate and the nation's consumer price index for the most recent 12-month period. This combination was a simple way to measure the level of "pain" or "misery" of the American people when it came to the overall level of joblessness and the loss of purchasing power due to rising inflation.

The misery index was first made politically newsworthy by Democratic presidential candidate Jimmy Carter in 1976. During the presidential election of that year, Mr. Carter constantly attacked President Gerald Ford for his mishandling of the American economy.

Candidate Carter frequently noted during the campaign that the misery index was in the mid-teens, as compared to much lower levels during the 1950s, 1960s, and early 1970s. Mr. Carter's criticism of President Ford's economic mismanagement was effective, helping him defeat the incumbent Republican president during the November 1976 election.

"What Goes Around..."

...comes around" as the saying goes. During the 1980 presidential campaign four years later, Republican candidate Ronald Reagan constantly made reference to President Carter's economic failings—as measured by Carter's misery index.

By November 1980, the misery index had moved even higher, with several monthly measurements above 20. Candidate Reagan's constant battering of President Carter with his own index turned out to be effective as Reagan handily defeated the incumbent Democratic president.

References to the misery index have clearly waned in recent years, although it remains a reasonable—if simplistic—measure of the

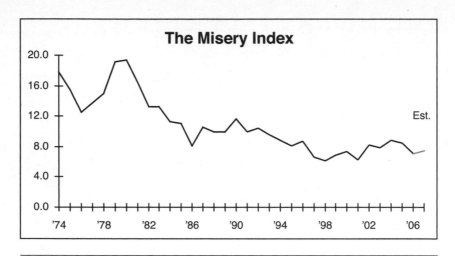

FIGURE 1.2 Misery Index

Source: Based on data from the U.S. Bureau of Labor Statistics.

American consumer's economic well-being. As Figure 1.2 shows, the United States made enormous progress in reducing this particular measure of consumer pain, especially during the decade of the 1990s.

The Numbers

On the employment side of the equation, impressive U.S. economic growth and resultant strong job creation during much of the past 10 years led the nation's unemployment rate to average 4.1 percent during calendar years 1999 and 2000, its lowest annual average in 30 years. The nation's unemployment rate actually fell slightly below 4.0 percent during various months in 2000, the lowest monthly rate since January 1970. While true, one actually has to go back to the mid-1950s to find a *peacetime* unemployment rate as low as 3.9 percent.

More recently, the nation's unemployment rate again declined from the near 6.0 percent average following the mild 2000 to 2001 recession. The 4.6 percent average in 2006 was its lowest average level in five years.

On the inflation side, pressures remained modest in the first years of the 21st century due to (1) fierce domestic and global competition in nearly every major industry; (2) more aggressive actions by consumers to resist price increases; (3) more effective corporate utilization of technology, and (4) the inflation-fighting nature of the Internet.

The escalation of numerous commodity prices during the 2004 to mid-2006 period led inflation pressures higher. Global prices for oil, steel, copper, lead, aluminum, and the like, tied in part to sharply rising demand from China and India, led overall inflation pressures higher before easing in late 2006. Such upward pressure on commodity prices was a key ingredient in the Federal Reserve's elongated monetary tightening program of June 2004 through June 2006.

Bottomed Out?

Has the misery index bottomed? Very likely. The nation's unemployment rate dipped to extremely low levels in 1998 to 2000. This decline was particularly impressive in light of frequent cost reduction and layoff programs regularly announced by prominent U.S. companies during the late 1990s. Inflation pressures were also largely muted during 1997 to 2003. The misery index will enter the history books as an interesting political footnote.

STATE OF THE STATES

The current U.S. economic expansion, now into its sixth year, has contributed to varying levels of performance among the 50 states. The simplistic comparison suggests that states in the West and the South have enjoyed stronger performance, while those in the Northeast and the Midwest have seen less robust economic growth.

Many states with significant natural resources including oil, natural gas, and coal are doing well. Many states more dependent on manufacturing are struggling.

The Rocky Mountain region leads the way in employment growth. By comparison, much of the region was hit very hard by the recession of 2000 to 2001; the events of September 11, 2001; and the initially weak U.S. economic recovery.

Conversely, the nation's industrial heartland of Indiana, Michigan, Ohio, and parts of the Northeast finds itself in the bottom 10 states as measured by employment gains, accompanied by Louisiana and Mississippi (hurricane impact). The primary culprit in the industrial Midwest has been ongoing job cuts in the auto sector and various auto suppliers.

Buddy, Can You Spare a Worker?

Extremely tight labor markets will contribute to some slowing in the high-growth states over the next 24 months. It is extremely difficult to fill open positions in numerous markets around the nation, including the Rocky Mountain states, the Upper Midwest, and Florida.

Various employers, including many in the construction, education, health care, natural resources, and transportation sectors, have publicized thousands of open positions with little, if any, response. Employers in various industries are paying signing bonuses for new hires or providing bonuses to current workers who bring in another potential employee.

More Revenue, Less Borrowing

Solid U.S. economic performance has led to a majority of the states (more than 40 at last count) now running budget surpluses. Many states are dealing with the greatest surge in tax revenue ever recorded.

Many states that suffered from serious budget challenges two to four years ago are now flush with new money.

A number of states are primarily spending excess revenues. Other states are returning a significant share of the revenue surpluses to taxpayers. State and local economic growth is clearly subject to fits and starts. Those state legislators who choose to primarily spend excess revenues, and largely commit taxpayers to higher spending in the future, may rue the day. States that cut income tax rates in times of excess revenue typically have greater levels of job and income creation versus those that ramp up current and future spending.

It's not rocket science.

CHAPTER 2

——EMPLOYMENT——

U.S. EMPLOYMENT

The Fear of 15 to 20 Years Ago

The issue of domestic labor availability has become increasingly critical during the past decade. This issue of extremely tight U.S. labor markets is all the more remarkable when one looks back to a largely unspoken—but major—source of political anxiety during the mid- to late 1980s.

The primary worry at that time? With all of the layoffs, "downsizing," and "rightsizing" taking place across the American economy impacting both skilled and unskilled people, a key question was "How will the country deal politically with the likelihood of millions of permanently unemployed people for years to come?"

That concern ended up dead wrong. The layoffs and job cuts of the mid- to late 1980s contributed to the U.S. economic strength of the 1990s and of recent years. Hundreds of thousands of displaced workers eventually started their own firms or joined small- and medium-sized companies.

The "animal spirits" and "entrepreneurial zeal" discussed in economics textbooks were unleashed. The result was the evolution of the most powerful, most competitive, and most dominant U.S. economic role in the world since the 1950s.

The end result also included a return to full employment across the American economy. The jobless rate averaged a low 4.9 percent during the 10-year period 1997 to 2006, lower than average jobless rates in the 1970s, 1980s, and 1990s as shown in Figure 2.1.

Today's tighter labor market reality includes the stress felt by employers of all shapes and sizes regarding the difficulty and—sometimes—inability to fill open positions. Smaller employers in

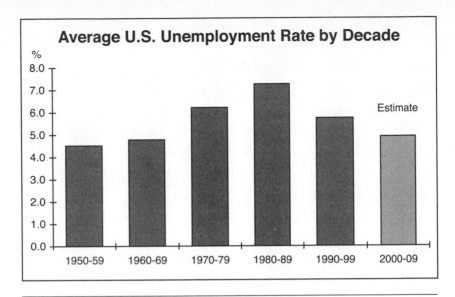

FIGURE 2.1   Average Unemployment Rate by Decade

Source: Based on data from the U.S. Bureau of Labor Statistics.

particular are also fearful of losing their most talented and valued workers to other employers.

Older Workers

A major American opportunity in coming years will be to retain a greater share of older workers in the labor force. The traditional American mentality that once a worker reaches the age of 60 or 65 they are ready to be "put out to pasture" must change. Fortunately, extremely tight labor availability expected in coming years will see this worn-out view displaced.

Likewise, Social Security income limitation rules were finally modified in 2000. The old rules had penalized workers between 65 and 69 years of age with partial loss of benefits if their earnings from wages and salaries exceeded $17,000 annually. Older workers are now much more willing to retain one foot (or both) in the working world if each dollar they earn contributes to their current financial support and retirement nest egg.

Has this change had any impact? The number of employed men and women age 55 and older has grown sharply in recent years.

The reasons why? The first is that the older members of the Baby Boom generation are now part of that group. The second reason is that many workers saw their retirement funds take a hit during the painful stock market washout of 2000 to 2002, forcing many to now supplement their incomes. Other older workers have found promised health care and pension benefits from major American corporations trimmed in recent years, necessitating a return to the workforce.

A fourth reason is that many early retirees found "retirement" a bit boring after a while. This factor will contribute to a major change in coming years. Various surveys suggest that a large majority of Baby Boomers do not plan to fully retire at or near age 65, but desire a balanced life of keeping one foot in the workforce while also having the time to enjoy travel, hobbies, sports and recreation, the grandkids, and the like.

More and more corporations are also targeting retirees as ideal part- or full-time workers. Various companies note the extremely low turnover rate of older workers and the minimal amount of training needed versus much younger workers.

Labor Concerns in Coming Years

The issue of extremely tight labor availability is not just a short-term concern. The Bureau of Labor Statistics forecasts the U.S. labor force is expected to grow at slightly below a 1 percent annual pace during the next 20 to 30 years, its slowest growth pace ever. The white male—the traditional entrant to the U.S. labor market—will represent roughly one out of every eight new entrants to the labor force in coming decades.

The flow of women into the American labor force since 1970 is largely complete, with the labor participation rate of women not expected to rise significantly further. The primary entrant to U.S. labor markets during the next 20 to 30 years will be minorities— both domestic and foreign, both legal and illegal. As a result, employers will have the opportunity to tap their respective talents as never before.

Layoffs

Layoffs by corporations have declined in recent years as a majority of American companies have enjoyed solid business activity. However, a number of companies in a variety of industries, especially in the automotive sector, continue to lay off extra workers or offer buyouts to those they wish to remove from bloated employment rolls.

A positive development tied to these job cuts is that other companies enjoying growth are in many cases snapping up these downsized (and skilled) people, especially in the small business area. For example, the unemployment rate for managers and professional employees was near 2.0 percent in early 2007 (U.S. Bureau of Labor Statistics).

Small companies have been the primary source of U.S. job creation strength during the past 20 years. Smaller employers remain eager to hire talented employees let go by larger companies in transition. The United States easily retains its position as the world's most powerful job creation machine among developed nations. Global envy of U.S. job creation capability remains intact.

The national media's fixation on all things negative, including job cut and job buyout announcements, would have us believe that few new jobs are being created. In fact, many of the companies announcing job cuts are creating comparable numbers of jobs, or even more, in other corporate divisions.

Churning

Net U.S. employment gains have averaged 180,000 jobs monthly since 2004. However, the net addition figure masks enormous change within the employment sector.

During the past decade, the economy has experienced a higher level of "job churning" than perhaps ever before as outmoded business operations are terminated and new business opportunities are explored. The Bureau of Labor Statistics reports that more than four million workers are dismissed from jobs or leave jobs voluntarily each month. At the same time, an even larger number of people begin new jobs each month.

The national media also suggests all too frequently that the U.S. economy has and continues to lose high-skill, high-pay positions, forcing many of those laid off to obtain lesser-quality and lower-paying jobs in fast-food restaurants, retail trade, and in other service industries. This broad assertion is largely incorrect. In fact, the strongest areas of U.S. job creation during the past few years have occurred in many of the highest-skill, highest-pay job classifications, led by professional and business services, financial services, construction, health care, and government employment.

Sharing the Wealth

A positive development occurring within corporate America is the increasing number of workers who now "share the wealth" of corporate success. Nearly half of all American private-sector workers now own stock or have stock options in their respective companies. This share is expected to rise during the next 20 years as more firms offer workers both stock options and attractive employee stock ownership plans. The incentive? It is for companies to retain their best and brightest employees in an extremely tight labor market.

Companies have found that "employee owners" are more committed to company success. This result has proven especially true when employees are also given more input into the company decision-making process. Companies where employer-employee *cooperation* has replaced employer-employee *confrontation* have performed well in recent years. This more logical approach will also define the future.

Growth in Wages

Stronger real wage gains have occurred in recent years as companies compete to both replace and protect critical workers. Various measures of overall employee compensation during 2006 were the strongest in a decade.

Rising wages are obviously a favorable development for American workers, helping to offset higher energy costs. Stronger U.S. wage and benefit gains, should they continue, will help consumers maintain spending levels in coming years.

At the same time, stronger growth in wages is potentially inflationary as various companies attempt to "pass through" higher wage costs to consumers and other firms in the form of higher prices. A variety of firms, particularly those where transportation costs are a significant component of doing business—such as airlines and trucking firms—have had success in passing through higher energy costs to their customers via fuel surcharges.

How to offset rising wages besides raising prices? Solid gains in worker productivity have been—and remain—the key.

America versus Europe

One of the most amazing comparisons regarding global job creation contrasts the United States with Europe. While the U.S. unemployment rate averaged 4.9 percent during 1997 through 2006, unemployment across Europe was nearly twice as high.

Job creation? The United States added more than 40 million net additional private-sector jobs since 1980, while the European Community added dramatically fewer new jobs.

A major reason? The "entry and exit" of workers is a reasonably painless process in the U.S. economy. Companies can add or eliminate workers with minimal disruption and limited government interference. The action might not always be pretty, but it works.

In contrast, once a company adds workers in many European countries, particularly France and Germany, powerful unions and outdated government-mandated employment rules can make it extremely difficult—and costly—to ever eliminate excess workers.

The reality among rational European employers? More overtime for current workers, if necessary, and more manufacturing production shifted to less costly locations such as Hungary, Poland, the Czech Republic, and Malaysia. European companies exercise extreme caution before hiring *any* new European-based workers.

A casualty? Hundreds of thousands of European youth are denied a chance to "show what they can do" in the workplace, with many remaining on the public dole for years to come.

Fortunately, some of these antiquated European employment rules are finally biting the dust. More insightful union leaders across Europe are recognizing the merits of increased employer-employee flexibility in the employment arena.

Education and Unemployment

As one would logically expect, higher levels of U.S. educational attainment are closely connected to higher levels of employment in an increasingly sophisticated American economy—and vice versa. The jobless rate for those with less than a high school diploma was 5.8 percent in early 2007. The jobless rate for high school graduates (with no college credit) was 4.2 percent in early 2007. The jobless rate for workers with some college or an associate's degree was 3.5 percent, while the jobless rate for those with a bachelor's degree or higher was below 2 percent.

Changing Labor Force in the Future

In addition to older workers representing a rising share of the workforce, employment success in the future will be tied more than ever before to worker flexibility. Long-term relationships between many employers and employees continue to decline. As a result, many future workers will adopt a "contract mentality," including beginning and completing a task and then moving on to the next project (and perhaps a new employer).

Traditional relationships between American workers and numerous U.S. employers who were known to provide lifelong employment were severely tarnished during the past 10 to 20 years—the downsizing and rightsizing process saw to that. However, a significant return to earlier times is in the works.

Many employers have become traumatized in recent years due to extremely tight labor availability. Such employers are increasingly anxious about losing their best and brightest employees. The result has been a rising corporate commitment to study what factors motivate valued employees to remain on the job as well as what factors enhance the quality of work or service provided by those employees.

More and more companies are also recognizing the direct correlation between satisfied employees—who provide higher-quality work or service—and the ultimate impact upon company profitability. Part of this development is a rising corporate recognition that in the knowledge-based economy of the 21st century, it is human capital—employees—that are of the greatest value, not brick-and-mortar facilities.

Progressive employers are now recognizing that their future success is increasingly tied to the stability and productivity of their

SILVER BULLET #1: TIGHT U.S. LABOR MARKETS

On balance, extremely tight U.S. labor markets expected during the next 20 years will sharply increase the real (inflation-adjusted) earnings of tens of millions of American workers, while also enhancing the value of their benefit and retirement programs. Successful companies in all industries and of all sizes will strive to minimize costly employee turnover and reward key employees.

This is a critical and major departure from labor conditions that existed during most of the past 20 years. This issue is the first of four major developments, referred to as Silver Bullets, that drive my optimistic view of the American economy in coming years.

respective workforces. Companies seeking to maintain top-quality workers on the payroll, while also seeking top talent, will provide them with more valuable and more flexible benefits. The move of many American companies to downsize the value and variety of benefits will decline sharply over the next 20 years.

The trend of replacing "defined benefit" pension programs with "defined contribution" plans will also continue. However, the financial incentives provided by enlightened companies for their employees to participate in 401(k), stock option, and other investment programs will be very attractive.

A MINIMUM WAGE

Few topics invite as much passion and emotion on both sides of the issue as a mandated increase in the nation's minimum wage. The nation's minimum wage was boosted in early 2007. The wage is scheduled to rise in three 70-cent increments over the next two years to reach $7.25 hourly in early 2009 (assumed at press time).

The minimum wage had been fixed at $5.15 per hour since September 1997. Over that nine-year-plus period, the purchasing power of that $5.15 per hour had fallen by 25 percent. The minimum wage would need to have reached $6.50 hourly in early 2007 to match the purchasing power of $5.15 in 1997.

The politics involved in the minimum wage discussion tend to follow political party mantra, with Republicans largely against a mandated increase. The Democrats favored a sizable upward adjustment.

As U.S. Department of Labor data shows, an estimated 1.9 million American workers (less than 2.5 percent of hourly paid workers, down sharply from 13.9 percent in 1979) are paid at the minimum wage or lower. Restaurant waiters, for example, are many times paid less, with the ability to receive tips to augment their incomes. Many minimum wage or less workers are young people, working part-time hours as they attend school.

The Argument against a Boost

Many Republicans, as well as more conservative-leaning groups and pro-business advocates such as the U.S. Chamber of Commerce, opposed a mandated increase. They argued that such a rise would actually lead to declining employment. The argument is that if employers, especially smaller employers, are forced to pay a minimum wage such as $6.75 or $7.25 hourly, they might choose to employ fewer people or allow fewer hours to be worked in order to limit overall wage costs.

Teen unemployment? It was already in excess of 15 percent in early 2007, with the African-American teen unemployment rate exceeding 28 percent. The argument continues that by depriving younger workers of the opportunity for that first job, the workforce skills necessary for advancement to higher wage levels are never learned, leading to even higher levels of public assistance and/or crime levels in subsequent years.

The Argument for a Boost

Many Democrats, as well as many "enlightened" community leaders, strongly favored a higher minimum wage. Advocates suggest that any total employment decline tied to a higher minimum wage is a fallacy. Advocates argue that the minimum wage must move higher in order to keep pace with the rise in the cost of living of recent years.

Republicans many times challenge the "no-impact" view voiced by Democrats, noting that if a $2.10 per hour or so rise will not impact hiring levels, why not a $5.00 or $10.00 increase in the minimum wage?

Ouch!

Many activist state and community leaders have mandated sharply higher minimum wage levels in recent years, noting the inability of the Congress to step up to the plate. Nearly half of the states already have a higher minimum wage.

Employers in many states face minimums ranging from $5.70 to $7.50 per hour. High-cost-of-living areas including Santa Fe, New Mexico, and San Francisco, California, have even higher minimum wage levels of $8.50 to $9.50 hourly.

The Realities

Many communities and states with higher minimum wage levels also provide exemptions for smaller employers. For example, while the minimum wage in Santa Fe is a lofty $9.50 per hour, companies with fewer than 25 employees (those most likely to offer lower wages and lesser-valued benefits) are exempt. Human nature suggests that many small companies in Santa Fe whose total employment is rapidly approaching the magic number of 25 workers will cap employment—or split the company into two or more entities—to avoid the mandated higher wage.

One factor that has made the minimum wage issue somewhat moot in many communities is the shortage of labor, which has forced wages higher. The national unemployment rate averaged 4.6 percent in 2006, the lowest level in five years. A U.S. Bureau of Labor Statistics projection that the U.S. labor force will grow at less than a 1 percent annual rate in coming years—the slowest growth pace ever—should keep labor markets extremely tight, helping to boost wages across the income spectrum.

Many of us who might inquire about the beginning wage at a fast food restaurant in many American locations would find that it is $6.50 to $7.50 or more hourly. Finding potential employees at $5.15 hourly?

Not a chance.

At the Polls

Democrats in many states and communities have taken a page from the opposition party. Republicans worked hard in recent national elections to bring emotional issues, such as the definition of marriage, to the November polls in order to draw a strong conservative turnout.

Democrats have pushed to place the minimum wage issue on ballots in order to draw supporting voters. A number of states actually saw Republican-controlled legislatures lead their state's minimum wage higher.

By doing so, Republicans could potentially nullify an even larger increase from being passed. In addition, such a Republican-induced increase might lessen the emotional need of many Democrats to vote in coming elections.

My View

This issue is largely one where the market will work. An extremely tight American labor market in coming years will boost real wages across the income spectrum in order for companies to be adequately staffed.

Note: As part of the Baby Boom generation, I entered the part-time workforce in 1967. The issue at that time was an enormous excess of workers of or near my age, with many, many fewer workplace opportunities (i.e., many fewer fast-food restaurants).

The minimum wage at that time was $1.40 per hour with an upward adjustment to $1.60 in 1968. When I think of all the hours that I worked at those wage levels!

The minimum wage did need to be increased—that much is clear. An upward adjustment, phased in over two years to $7.25 hourly, seems fair and affordable. What happens after that as far as future adjustments creates another problem.

The minimum wage debate is one that will continue to draw intense emotion and a mix of both good and bad "evidence" to support a point of view. A somewhat similar issue is in the political mainstream and draws only limited emotion as to how to regularly boost benefits—Social Security cost-of-living increases.

Imagine the political nonsense and demagoguery if annual adjustments to Social Security payments were a political football. The issue is moot because annual adjustments are automatically tied to the rise in consumer prices.

Following the scheduled increases, the same approach is a good idea for the minimum wage as well.

OUTSOURCING

Emotion concerning the loss of American "blue collar" manufacturing jobs to low-wage nations has been center stage for years. Jobs lost in the auto sector, textiles, tires, electronics, and other industries have hurt total manufacturing employment in this country.

More recently, the same development has occurred in traditional white collar occupations such as telephone call centers, accounting, tax preparation, brokerage industry research, claims adjustment, home loan processing, engineering, product research, law, architecture, and the like. Projections of additional job losses in coming years have raised awareness further. Worst-case fears frequently portrayed by the national media see America eventually becoming a nation of "hamburger flippers" as we lose first our industrial base, followed by our professional occupations.

The opposing view presents the idea that such changes are both part and parcel of an expanded global economy. America is losing neither its ability to "make things" nor its ability to compete effectively in a dynamic and enormously competitive global marketplace.

The Losses: Blue Collar

It is no secret that the United States has lost significant numbers of manufacturing jobs over the past 20 years to other nations. Jobs that originally went to Mexico or the Caribbean have now, in many cases, relocated again to China. As the common wisdom suggests, the cost of production is so low in China that American firms simply cannot compete on a price basis.

Based on U.S. Bureau of Labor Statistics data, the United States has lost roughly three million manufacturing jobs in the past seven years alone. Such losses equate to one of every six manufacturing jobs that existed in this country in 2000. While some outsourcing of manufacturing jobs has clearly taken place, the vast majority of lost manufacturing employment has been tied to powerful gains in worker productivity in recent years. In fact, no sector of the American economy has experienced more impressive gains in worker productivity during the past few years than has American manufacturing.

Why are productivity gains so important? More efficient and more productive workers let employers pay higher wages without having to pass these higher costs on to the consumer in the form of higher prices. Rising productivity gains are a prime ingredient in raising the standard of living for American families.

The Losses: White Collar

Concerns about the loss of white collar jobs are high. Many of these professional jobs will relocate to India to join thousands already there. College graduates are available in India by the tens of thousands, although labor markets are tightening and wage levels are climbing rapidly. Most of these workers are fluent in English and are known for a solid work ethic.

Indian wage levels run about 20 percent to 40 percent less than American wage levels for the same skills. American firms suggest they simply cannot be competitive in a cutthroat global marketplace if they do not take advantage of these savings. Many American companies note the cost savings in India and elsewhere provide the ability to boost wage levels for remaining workers in the United States. Company managers note that outsourcing is a reality in remaining competitive in the global community.

The United States has not been alone in losing jobs to less costly places. Percentage losses of manufacturing jobs in particular have been significantly higher in recent years in Great Britain, Japan, and especially in Germany.

One other development likely to gain speed is the outsourcing of various U.S. jobs to South America. Various Central and South American nations will try to attract U.S. jobs intended for or having already moved to India. Such nations can offer three positive factors that are not found in India.

The first is the closer proximity to the United States, where a company official can quickly reach a nation only hours away. A second factor is that the time zones are nearly identical to those in the United States, as opposed to time zones 12 or more hours different across India. The third factor is the rising financial clout of the Hispanic and Latino population in the United States. Such U.S. customers will be most comfortable dealing with people who in most cases speak the same languages.

Returning Home

The national media would have one believe that outsourcing is a one-way street. Such is not the case. Numerous examples exist of American companies bringing jobs back to the United States after an outsourcing venture provided less than was expected. Other companies have canceled plans to outsource.

Some companies note that cost savings were not as expected, while others note that the loss of operational control halfway around the world was not acceptable. The United States also continues to attract new investment and new jobs from around the world, especially from foreign automakers. This two-way flow of jobs is expected to continue in coming years.

The Flip Side

We tend to view China, India, and other developing countries as nations looking only to steal U.S. and other nations' manufacturing (and now) professional jobs. We tend to forget that these nations also represent vast markets of opportunity for American consumer goods, industrial equipment, travel, and entertainment.

China and India alone represent more than one-third of the world's population. As more high-quality jobs are created in those countries, wages will climb, standards of living will rise, and their citizens' appetites for Western goods and services will skyrocket. Are American companies adequately taking advantage of these opportunities?

Enormous changes will continue to occur. More jobs will leave American, European, and Japanese soil. However, other markets will develop. Those companies that take advantage of trends already under way and see new markets of opportunity will prosper. Those that do not will simply bite the dust.

SMALL BUSINESS IN AMERICA

The nation's largest companies get the lion's share of media attention. However, the amazing U.S. job growth of the past 15 years has taken place primarily within small and medium-sized businesses.

A greater and greater share of the American economy is comprised of small businesses. Downsizing efforts and layoff programs of Fortune 500 companies have been commonplace since the 1980s, with a net overall reduction in Fortune 500 employment over the past two decades. This change has occurred even as profitability of American corporations is at record levels.

America's small businesses number in the millions. A case could be made that the collective size and economic might of America's small business community would rival the size of any other nation's economy on the planet.

Underestimated

Official U.S. employment data each month results from a monthly survey of roughly 375,000 medium- and large-sized businesses. In contrast, the nation's unemployment rate comes from a monthly survey of 60,000 households, with frequent changes in those households surveyed. This survey has an employment component as well.

With respect to overall job creation, the two surveys typically tell similar stories as more time passes and as more complete data is available. Revisions to the data can be substantial.

In recent years, however, the differential in employment gains between the two surveys has been enormous. During recent five-year periods, the household survey reported nearly twice as many net new jobs created as the "official" survey.

The national media's focus on all things negative has constantly told us that we have suffered through a jobless recovery in recent years.

I beg to differ.

Small Business Growth

What the data tells me is that a greater share of new jobs being created involves consultants, contract workers, 1099 workers, and the like. The data also tells me that more and more small businesses are being created—and more and more existing small businesses are adding new workers—than ever before. These jobs *are not* included in the survey of medium- and large-sized businesses. These jobs *are* counted in the monthly survey of households.

The Demographics

Demographic changes will impact the small business sector in a huge way in coming years. Most current small business owners who are soon to retire are white males. Many of these existing businesses will eventually be acquired by women and minorities, expanding the already growing economic clout of each.

Rural communities have benefited greatly as the Internet provides instantaneous communication from almost anywhere. Many communities formerly dependent upon natural resource extraction and agriculture are now reinventing themselves as technology hubs.

Advantages

One advantage of smaller employers is the greater opportunity for people to develop their skills in a broad range of areas. Employees typically feel a greater sense of accomplishment. Providing immediate feedback, giving unexpected rewards, and strengthening benefits programs can be powerful tools in retaining quality talent once on board.

Another advantage of small business is a greater awareness of worker needs. Smaller employers usually have greater flexibility in scheduling work hours, helping to keep more workers content. Older workers may also find more flexibility and fulfillment with smaller companies.

The outlook for small business is bright. The Internet and technology allow small companies to be serious players in many markets. Access to capital has also risen sharply in recent years.

The future of the American business landscape—is small business.

CHAPTER 3

GOVERNMENT

TAXES

Few topics draw as much debate and contention in the political arena as do tax rates. Advocates and critics of lower tax rates draw different conclusions from the same data. However, the evidence is quite clear:

Lower tax rates lead to rising tax revenue in most cases.

Higher tax rates lead to lower tax revenue in most cases.

Three Times

Post–World War II history has provided three specific examples of overall tax-cut programs leading to rising tax revenue. The first was under Democratic President John F. Kennedy, who promoted and helped pass tax cuts in the early 1960s. Lower tax rates at that time helped to unleash the "animal spirits" and incentives that drive U.S. economic performance.

The result? Higher tax revenue.

The second major example was of tax cuts proposed and enacted under Republican President Ronald Reagan in the 1980s. Despite the screams and wails of critics—primarily Democrats—the top marginal income tax rate was cut from 70 percent to as low as 28 percent.

The result? Given the power of additional incentives (lower tax rates) to earn, invest, and report income, overall tax revenues *doubled* during Reagan's eight years in office.

The third example was that of Republican President George W. Bush in recent years, who proposed and signed into law a series of both income and investment tax rate reductions. The evidence again resulted in powerful additions to overall tax revenue. In fact, the rise in overall tax revenue during fiscal years (FY) 2005 and 2006 of more than $500 billion (nearly 15 percent annually) was the largest two-year rise ever recorded.

Critics of the Bush tax cuts of recent years decried the fact that wealthy taxpayers received much more in net tax reductions (as measured in actual dollars) than did lower-income earners. The nature of across-the-board tax cuts provides such a result.

What the Democrats Want

Democrats favor any form of tax policy that increases overall taxes paid by the wealthy, with favored tax policy finding high-income earners paying a larger share of total tax revenue. In this case, they should love the Bush tax cuts!

The surge in high-income earners' tax payments has been substantial in recent years. Out of every 100 Americans, the three wealthiest taxpayers are now paying close to the same amount in taxes as the other 97 taxpayers combined! Isn't that what the Democrats want?

Perhaps the critics of major tax cuts could lessen the hysteria about giveaways to the rich and pay more attention to the data.

It is no surprise that reductions in income tax rates led to higher tax revenue from the wealthy. However, the reductions in capital gains and dividend tax rates were even more powerful and even greater in support of the Democratic logic of "taxing the rich."

Between 2002 and 2004, capital gains tax revenues surged by 79 percent, AFTER the capital gains tax rate was reduced from 20 percent to 15 percent. In addition, tax revenue from dividends paid on stocks jumped 35 percent during the same two-year period, after the tax rate was REDUCED from as high as 39.6 percent to 15 percent.

Comparable gains in new tax revenue were also recorded in FY2005 and FY2006, helping lead the budget deficit to annual declines. Such tax flow realities strongly support the idea that numerous tax cuts of recent years due to expire in 2010 must be made permanent.

20 Years Ago

A totally opposite but entirely consistent development occurred in the mid-1980s. The tax rate on capital gains was cut to 20 percent in the early 1980s as part of the Reagan tax cuts.

Bowing to intense political pressure in his second term, President Reagan reluctantly agreed to a series of tax hikes. One of these was for the capital gains tax rate to be hiked to 28 percent from the existing 20 percent rate, effective January 1, 1987.

Capital gains tax revenue was extremely high in 1986's final quarter. Public-sector tax revenue forecasters were gleeful as they prepared tax revenue projections for 1987.

The common wisdom in government, particularly at the state level was, "Wow! If we generated such high revenues in 1986's final few months at a 20 percent tax rate, just imagine the tax revenue that will arrive at a 28 percent rate!"

You guessed it. Capital gains tax revenue fell by two-thirds from that of the prior year. The reason? People make rational and intelligent decisions about their financial situation in most cases. Maybe someday, various government entities across the nation will figure that out.

Tax cuts leave more dollars in taxpayers' pockets. These additional dollars are then invested and spent, with both actions leading to rising economic activity.

As I will mention ad nauseum in this book, the most simple and most complete definition of economics is "people respond to incentives." No stronger incentives exist than lower tax rates, especially on investment income.

A Problem with Static

One problem in government analysis of tax-cut or tax-increase programs is the fact that "static" analysis is used. What this means is that government computer models of projected tax revenue assume that people do not make any changes in their spending or investment decisions as far as tax changes are involved.

As a result, a lower tax rate "officially" projects that lower tax revenue will arise. In addition, a projected tax increase will lead tax revenue higher. Most private-sector forecasting tools have adopted "dynamic" analysis, which logically assumes that American consumers and investors will modify their financial actions to take advantage of, or minimize the pain of, significant changes in tax rates.

Americans make rational decisions about money in most cases. The government has yet to figure that out. Effective tax policy does make a difference!

The Estate Tax

Emotional debate regarding "the death tax" is commonplace in the nation's capital. Republicans decry the idea that the government should tax an estate at the death of the owner, while Democrats see such taxation as entirely fair and appropriate. The reality is that the U.S. taxes death at one of the highest rates in the world, with many nations favoring zero taxation.

While Democrats and Republicans push their polarized views, there is a middle ground that appeals to the more moderate elements in both parties. Such middle ground also receives considerable support among the American people.

Like the emotional debate regarding the minimum wage, both parties stake out far right and far left positions. Effective government is supposed to be the art of compromise.

Prior to legislative changes in 2001, estates of as little as $1 million were taxed as high as 55 percent. Such a confiscatory tax rate had no place in the American free enterprise system.

The estate tax has traditionally applied to only about one percent of U.S. taxpayers. Legislation passed in 2001 provided for a sizable rise in the amount subject to exemption each year, while also providing for reductions in tax rates over time. Such changes will lessen the share of taxpayers subject to the estate tax in coming years.

One flaw in the current legislation is that after totally disappearing in 2010, the estate subject to taxation and the tax rate will return to pre-2001 levels. Legislators during 2001 presumably sought a passable compromise, with improvements to be worked out at some future time.

In a perfect world, taxation of estates of any size would not occur. Critics of such taxation argue that the death tax is immoral as the money has already been taxed once or twice, if not even three times. It is not a perfect world. What is viable and reasonable in the hands of Republicans is unfair and sacrilegious to Democrats.

The truth is that most estates will never be taxed. A broad compromise similar to the following framework is likely to emerge from the Congress in coming years.

Perhaps the first $4 to $6 million of an estate would avoid taxation. Larger estates might find the next $15 to $20 million taxed at around 15 percent to 19 percent, while still larger estates would be taxed at near a 30 percent rate.

Estate tax policy must appear fair to the American people. Given the high level of emotion on both sides of the political aisle, the art of compromise is the only avenue to new legislation in coming years.

Let's get on with it.

GOVERNMENT SPENDING

Only in the nation's capital can politicians "cut spending" and still spend billions *more* than the year before. How is this possible?

Accounting in Washington, D.C., works like nowhere else in the world. Government programs are driven by baseline projections, which project spending higher and higher year after year.

For example, if a program spent $500 million one year, the baseline appropriation for the following year might be $540 million. If the Congress trims that appropriation from $540 million to $525 million, the Congress takes credit for a $15 million spending cut—even though spending in that program just increased by $25 million.

Any wonder how we ended up $9 trillion in debt?

Even as government revenues have risen sharply over the past few years, government spending growth has been excessive. Yes, much of the increase was tied to the "war on terror," with hundreds of billions of dollars spent in Afghanistan and Iraq.

However, the level of "pork barrel" spending under Republican control in recent years has been a travesty. Fiscal responsibility has traditionally been a hallmark of the Republican party. Unfortunately, Republicans of the 21st century have clearly ignored their history to their elective peril.

All too much of the budget, now approaching $3.0 trillion annually, is associated with mandated or nondiscretionary spending increases such as more spending each year for Social Security, interest on the national debt, Medicare, Medicaid, and so forth. A smaller share of total government spending is debated within the halls of Congress.

While the alarming growth of nondiscretionary spending must be addressed in coming years, the irresponsible growth rate in discretionary spending has been a travesty. A solid and distasteful example of a lack of spending restraint was the energy bill passed in 2005.

Laden with Pork

The energy bill did very little in the way of moving this nation away from energy dependence on hostile and potentially hostile sources of oil in the coming decades. What it did have was an estimated

$20 billion of "pork" associated with it in more than 6,000 earmarks. These individual spending items did little for the nation but looked good to constituents at home.

Political tradition usually found pork projects added to a bill at the last minute. Fiscally responsible members would many times catch these abuses and attempt to have them excluded.

That changed. Horse-trading between members of Congress found little in the way of restraint, limited challenges to other projects by members of Congress, and a near "feeding frenzy" as to who could add the most pork spending to a bill.

Such irresponsible spending led by Republicans eventually spelled their leadership demise in the Congress. The Democratic Congress that took control in early 2007 will hopefully give greater consideration to spending restraint.

Spending restraint will grow much more intimidating in coming years as spending growth in government entitlement programs forces difficult decisions to be made in the nation's capital. Ignoring such choices will be to our combined detriment as tens of millions of Baby Boomers reach retirement age over the next 20 years.

BUDGET DEFICITS

One positive by-product of an enormous surge of tax revenue into Washington in recent years has been a series of smaller federal budget deficits. The administration proudly noted that the budget deficit for FY2006 (which ended on September 30, 2006) was $247 billion, according to the Office of Management and Budget (OMB).

Such a budget deficit was a far cry better than the OMB projection early in 2006 of a FY2006 deficit of $423 billion, a forecast that Democrats suggest was intentionally high in order to make more recent news look better. The Congressional Budget Office (CBO) had originally forecast a deficit of $345 billion. The FY2006 deficit also compared to the $318 billion shortfall in FY2005 and the $413 billion shortfall in FY2004.

The president trumpets the fact that the FY2006 deficit was roughly 1.9 percent of GDP (a $247 billion deficit as compared to $13 trillion in annual GDP), actually less than budget deficits during 17 of the past 25 years. The president also notes that his promise to cut the deficit in half by FY2008 would be reached even sooner.

Longer-term deficit projections of the two government forecasting bodies differ in coming years. The CBO forecast expects a modest decline from $247 billion in FY2006 to near $200 billion in FY2007, with growing deficits over the four following years. The administration's OMB projects a comparable deficit in FY2007, with deficits averaging less than 1 percent of GDP in FY2008 through FY2011. Most private-sector forecasters expect a FY2007 deficit around $200 billion.

Figments of Imagination

Gone are the old days (mostly the 1970s) when official government estimates of economic growth, inflation, job creation, budget deficits, and the like were released by a fictitious economist affectionately referred to as "Rosy Scenario." Forecasts in those days were always best-case scenarios, with little resemblance to reality.

Forecasts of recent administrations, while many times leaning slightly in a desired direction, are not typically far from private-sector views. Government credibility, at least in terms of economic and financial projections, is much higher than before.

Long-term economic growth and deficit forecasts become increasingly sketchy the further they are into the future. However, such forecasts become the basis for an administration's revenue and spending projections in coming years.

What Should Be

Unfortunately, history also tells us that the U.S. government should be running a budget surplus this far into an economic expansion. With solid U.S. economic growth and the nation's unemployment rate averaging below 5.0 percent since 2005, dollars flowing into Washington should exceed the dollars flowing out.

This is not the case.

Prior Surpluses

The Democrats boast that President Clinton oversaw a sizable budget surplus during the final four years of his reign, with a combined surplus of $559 billion in FY1998 through FY2001. They talk of the positive impact of a tax increase in Clinton's first term and spending restraint as the reasons why. The evidence tells a different story.

Budget deficits gave way to budget surpluses in President Clinton's second term because of strong U.S. economic growth and the surge of capital gains tax revenue resulting from sky-high stock prices in the late 1990s. The reality that Clinton had an opportunity to slash defense spending in the 1990s also contributed mightily to lesser spending and resulting budget surpluses.

The Long Run

One of the most powerful economic voices of the 20th century, British economist John Maynard Keynes, when questioned about his long-term views was known to reply, "In the long run, we are all dead." The consensus view of longer-term deficit pressures almost without exception notes enormous pressures on government spending and resultant deficits.

The reason? Under current legislation, huge increases in spending in coming decades on government "entitlement" programs of Social Security, Medicare, and Medicaid will occur, compliments of 78 million retiring Baby Boomers.

National politicians must soon reach agreement on a plan to reduce government spending growth rates in these programs. The alternative would be tax rate hikes or budget deficits that would be unpalatable to future taxpayers, as well as to financial market players who already buy boatloads of U.S. Treasury debt obligations. In my opinion, financial market pressures will force such difficult decisions to be made. See Silver Bullet #2 in Chapter 4.

THE POLITICS

In my 32 years of writing a weekly economic and financial newsletter, I have generally been reluctant to take one political party or another to task. I have favored a middle road to allow a more unbiased view of both political parties. When politics have been critical to potential economic developments, I have tried to be balanced and discussed views from the economic and/or financial perspective, leaving politics to others.

My political views have always leaned to the conservative side. I am a big fan of limited government—within reason, the smaller the better. I share the view of many that government creates as many problems as it solves.

Definition

As noted before, a simple and effective definition of economics is "people respond to incentives." I have always believed that cutting tax rates leads to rising tax revenues in most cases and that raising tax rates leads to a reduction in net revenue in most cases.

My conservative views have traditionally led me to favor Republican candidates for national office and to favor Republican control of the White House and the Congress. The traditional Republican aim was to limit the role of government, keep tax rates low, and require greater personal responsibility of individual citizens.

This mind-set also included concerns about Democrats being in power. The simplistic view was that Democrats had a stronger interest in spending money, with much of it coming from the rich to give to the poor.

Republicans were usually more willing to trumpet the latest tax cut or their role in keeping "government" under control. Democrats traditionally were more interested in spending money in order to tell the folks back home they were working for them.

No more.

My view became more clouded in recent years, with a rising distaste for politics in general—and a great disgust with Republican politics of recent years. I supported President Bush's tax cuts because I saw them providing more "incentive" for people to work hard, save and invest more, and be willing to report more income, with substantial tax revenues ultimately rolling in.

The Bush Administration

It is certainly clear that the major reason for the public's distaste with President Bush is the conflict in Iraq. Millions of voters, who initially might have supported our expansion of the "war on terror" into Afghanistan and Iraq, have become totally disillusioned with the seeming lack of progress that has resulted. Eliminating Saddam Hussein was one thing—a costly and painful effort at nation building is something else.

Voters tire at the more than $2 billion we spend each week in Iraq and elsewhere as we fight terrorism. We collectively hope that Iraqi forces will step up more diligently, and let American and coalition forces return home.

History will likely tarnish President Bush with the stain of Iraq. History will also give him credit and blame for two other major decisions.

Bush—the Positive

The tax cuts of a few years ago were, in my opinion, solid fiscal policy steps. I would argue that such cuts should be made permanent, especially those concerning a lower tax rate on dividends and capital gains.

Critics argued that tax cuts across the board benefited primarily the rich. No argument here. However, it is the rich who create jobs—it is also the rich who pay most of the taxes. Those who wish to see the wealthy pay even more in taxes should love developments of recent years.

Income tax revenue surged over the past few years, with most of the gain in revenue coming from the wealthy. Corporate income tax revenue has also surged as solid economic performance has contributed to strong growth in corporate profitability. Overall tax revenues have risen sharply to date in FY2007, on top of the record 25 percent cumulative rise in tax revenue during the prior two years.

Bush—the Negative

History will take President Bush to task for his unwillingness to impose spending restraint on the former Republican-led Congress. A U.S. president does not control the nation's purse strings but *does* have the ability to veto spending bills they see as irresponsible. This president had many opportunities to veto legislation laden with wasteful spending (pork) and chose not to do so.

History is also likely to be unkind to this president in regard to the Medicare prescription drug program passed in 2005. It would be difficult to find any similar program that will challenge our ability to pay for it in coming decades as does this costly and unnecessary program.

Fair Play

This president has never received a fair shake from the nation's media. It is no secret that the majority of the national media has a strong liberal bias. As a result, Republican policy initiatives are typically cast in a negative light, while any good news relative to the economy is relegated to the back pages.

President Bush has experienced even greater liberal distaste than other leaders during recent decades, as he was seen as one who did not occupy the White House legitimately. Democratic presidential candidate Al Gore received more votes in November 2000 and, in their view, should have run the show in recent years.

Veto Power

Late in President Bush's first term, I suggested to audience members, when the deficit question arose, that I thought President Bush would be very willing to veto pork-filled spending bills in his *second* term. I suggested he would do so, even though he was the first president serving a full term since John Quincy Adams (1825–1829) to not veto a single bill. Note: His summer 2006 veto of a stem cell research bill was his first use of veto power.

Why did I think he would veto bills? In a simplistic sense, to lessen the chance that history would paint him as one who took the "Clinton surpluses" and replaced them with irresponsible "Bush deficits" for as far as the eye could see.

His actions with the new Democratic Congress will determine whether I am right or wrong on the Bush veto call.

CHAPTER 4

ENTITLEMENT PROGRAMS

THE ENTITLEMENT ISSUE

No long-term issue is more challenging than the future funding of American entitlement programs. Millions of today's elderly people clamor for more spending. Others fear that spending cuts will eventually be implemented and simply want well enough left alone.

Millions of Baby Boomers are aware of the funding imbalance that is sure to unfold in coming decades, but hope that they can get in under the wire before changes are required. Millions of other Boomers vow to fight any current and future politicians who might tamper with their "right" to receive sizable government payments for decades to come.

Millions of younger workers bristle at the "me first" attitudes of their parents and grandparents as to government payments. Younger workers know that without substantial changes, future tax hikes needed to keep programs solvent will greatly impair their own abilities to prosper.

Many other Boomers, however, combined with millions of their parents, recognize the long-term financial fragility of these programs. They envision a time when responsible bipartisan politicians will modify programs to provide fairness today and viable funding for their children and grandchildren tomorrow.

These more enlightened taxpayers recognize that *spending cuts* will not be necessary in these programs (despite the emotional finger pointing by deceitful politicians), but simply reductions in future *growth rates* of spending. In addition, millions of younger workers will patiently recognize that, as they age, their generation will draw enough political support from their peers to rectify pending imbalances.

No Status Quo

Future funding pressures on the government's primary entitlement programs of Medicare, Medicaid, and Social Security are unavoidable.

The enormous size and assumed longevity of the Baby Boom generation provides no escape from the need to constrain the growth rates of future spending.

The three major programs all have rapid spending growth. Medicare and Medicaid expenditures have been rising at average annual rates of 9 percent or more annually, with similar growth projections in coming years. Such growth will lead to a doubling of spending in eight years or less, with another doubling eight years later, and so on. Note: Medicaid spending was essentially flat during FY2006, while Medicare spending rose roughly 12 percent from the prior year.

Social Security's spending growth is currently running at a lesser rate annually, but is assured to grow more rapidly as the oldest of the Boomers can begin to draw benefits in 2008. Spending growth thereafter will rise sharply.

Critics of these programs point out that the unfunded liability of these programs currently exceeds $84 trillion, with most of that in the Medicare arena, and with much tied to the new prescription drug program. Unfunded liability? This total represents the future commitment of promised benefits minus funds expected to be collected to pay such benefits.

Eighty-four trillion dollars ($84,000,000,000,000) is a difficult number to grasp. It currently equates to six times the annual output of the American economy.

The unavoidable truth is that the U.S. economy cannot grow fast enough to provide the necessary future funding for these programs. Solid U.S. economic growth, based on pro-growth and incentive-based tax and investment policies, will carry much of the battle. However, adjustments will have to be made. The sooner these adjustment are made, the less onerous and less disruptive they will be.

The poor relationship between Democrats and Republicans in the nation's capital does not lend itself to easy solutions. Any current politicians who dare speak the truth regarding the need to make difficult choices sooner rather than later are quickly branded by the political opposition as uncaring and spiteful toward the elderly.

Politicians of recent years have shied away from these difficult choices, simply leaving them for other politicians at other times. This "solution" is no longer viable. Looking back to another generation may provide a clue as to required political cooperation tomorrow.

Prior Cooperation

Social Security faced a funding crisis in the mid-1980s, with both major political parties in quiet agreement that something needed to be done. The bipartisan Greenspan Commission, chaired by future (and now former) Federal Reserve Chair Alan Greenspan, was created to study Social Security funding issues and make recommendations for long-term improvement.

The bipartisan recommendations that emerged provided meaningful improvement and fiscal solvency for decades to come, with most of the changes to take place in future years. A series of modest tax increases were phased in over a dozen years. In addition, the prior reality of full benefits at age 65 for all was stretched out. A later retirement age for Boomers was phased in, ranging from 65 years and two months up to age 67 for even later retirees.

SOCIAL SECURITY

One of President Bush's objectives during his second term has been to fix the Social Security "crisis." A key element of his proposed solution is to allow younger workers to withhold up to 25 percent of their FICA taxes and invest into individually owned retirement accounts. Younger people would then direct these funds over decades into stocks, bonds, mutual funds, and the like. This move would support his idea of an "ownership society."

SILVER BULLET #2: NAP TIME IS COMING

This nation will reach a point in coming years when politicians are simply forced by the pressure of powerful financial markets and by constant media attention to set aside political rancor and work together to solve the entitlement funding and benefit issue. We refer to this as *NAP* (No Alternative Politics) time.

Neither party will be willing then or able to make such changes alone. Strong political leadership will see a bipartisan commission created, with required program changes debated in a civil environment. The full Congress will likely be asked to approve changes as proposed by the study group, with no ability to make modifications. Members of both major political parties will agree to avoid finger pointing and accusations, recognizing that a cooperative effort is mandatory.

We have been at this point before and responded. We will do so again. We simply have no alternative. This issue is the second of four major developments, referred to as Silver Bullets, that drive my optimistic view of the American economy in coming years.

I have not favored this solution. In a perfect world, it might make sense to have individual retirement accounts. It is not a perfect world.

Too Much Borrowing

One of the hard realities of the president's proposal was for the U.S. Treasury to borrow up to $2 trillion over the next 10 years to "replace" tax revenue lost to the Social Security System with the creation of private accounts. These funds would no longer be available to pay current benefits. What you didn't hear about was the need for the U.S. Treasury to borrow an additional $3 trillion to offset the funding loss in the second 10-year period.

This is up to $5 trillion of additional borrowed money—additional debt. What this country doesn't need is $5 trillion in additional debt on top of the $9 trillion gross national debt already outstanding, especially when this suggestion does very little to fix Social Security.

The Social Security program is not broken. Pay-as-you-go funding will keep it in surplus for the next 10 to 15 years. The program can then tap into the "mythical" Social Security Trust Fund for the next 20 to 30 years, which is discussed in its own section in this chapter. These projections are based on conservative assumptions about future U.S. economic growth and job creation. U.S. economic growth is likely to be stronger.

Tinkering Around the Edges

What the Social Security program requires is some "tinkering around the edges" to make the program financially viable for future generations when funding pressures are more painful. These changes will require bipartisan cooperation.

My parents have each drawn Social Security for roughly 15 years. I tell them that Social Security funding is not an issue they need to worry about. As a Boomer, I will not draw full benefits until age 66. I tell my married kids that Social Security will be there for them, but not to plan on drawing it until they are 68, 69, or 70 years of age.

I favor proposals that stretch out the retirement age for younger people. This change reflects the reality that younger people will be able to work longer if they wish, will live longer, and will, correspondingly, draw Social Security payments longer.

A minor change in the inflation calculation used to determine initial benefit payments for higher-income earners is desirable. Such higher-income workers would have their future payment schedule inflation-adjusted by the change in consumer prices. Lower-income workers could continue to have initial payment levels inflation-adjusted by the average annual growth in wages, resulting in their getting a slightly better deal in the future than higher-income workers.

I would suggest a slightly faster boost in wages subject to current taxation. For example, the annual adjustment to the wage cap might be the change in consumer prices plus an additional 1 percent each year during the next decade.

Providing greater incentives for people to save for retirement is advisable. Additional or expanded programs like the 401(k) would help minimize the role played by Social Security for millions of future retirees.

A Savings Incentive

I would favor other incentives to boost retirement savings of lower-income families. If we are willing to go in debt another $5 trillion for the president's proposal, might we instead consider a two or three-to-one match for lower-income people? For every $1,000 saved for retirement by lower-income people, the government would match it with a $2,000 or $3,000 payment that would not be accessible until during retirement.

Changes such as these are required to strengthen Social Security for generations to come. The inclusion of personal accounts would also make sense, but only as part of a comprehensive program.

The Mythical Trust Fund

Responsible politicians talk today of Social Security changes required for the future. However, a major issue regarding Congressional misuse of Social Security surpluses of recent years has been largely neglected by the American people.

The following remarks are how I attempted during much of the past 18 years to get audiences to think about the Social Security funding issue and the need for legitimate investment of surplus revenue. The numbers used have been updated to the present.

One of my passions as an economist is Social Security—and it involves the funding of Social Security for the future. My parents both now draw Social Security. I tell them that in their lifetimes they have nothing to worry about relative to the long-term viability of Social Security.

I am a Baby Boomer—many of you are Baby Boomers. We, the Baby Boom generation, 78 million strong, and the generations that follow us have something to worry about.

Now you can ask your respective member of Congress for the status of Social Security and they will tell you a story:

- They will note that following the recommendations of the 1983 Greenspan Commission on Social Security, we engaged in a two-step process to ensure the viability of Social Security for the next 75 years. Between 1983 and 1995, we engaged in a series of payroll tax increases, now at 6.2 percent of wages—matched by our employers—on the first $97,500 of wages in 2007 (plus another 1.45 percent for Medicare with no earnings limit, also matched by our employers).

- Your respective member of Congress would tell you that Social Security today is running a surplus, which is true.

- They would tell you that the surplus in the most recent year was around $170 billion, which is true.

- They would tell you that projections call for surpluses averaging in excess of $180 billion per year during the next decade, which is also true.

- They would tell you that by law, the surplus funds *must* be invested into U.S. Treasury notes to be saved for the future, which is true.

- They would tell you that the current savings pool has more than $2 trillion of U.S. Treasury securities in it, with the intent of building a multitrillion-dollar trust fund for that point in coming years when the Baby Boom generation begins to retire.

- They would note that we will eventually reach a point—estimated to be around 2040—where we have two workers for each retiree, versus 3.2 workers for each retiree today. Compare that to the 16.5 workers for each retiree in 1950.

The funding pressures upon Social Security at that time will be enormous—we already know that. The intent in the future will be for the Social Security administrators to (figuratively) go to the back room, reach into a box, and pick up $200 billion or so of U.S. Treasury notes and walk them over to the U.S. Treasury Department to cash them in to help pay current benefits.

This is where the problem is.

Tell me this. Where will the U.S. Treasury get the money to redeem $200 billion, $250 billion, or $300 billion of U.S. Treasury Notes presented annually for redemption? The answer? The money does not exist. Where will the Treasury get it? The Treasury will do what it does best—borrow it.

The biggest charade, the biggest scam, the biggest deceit in Washington, D.C., is the fraudulent funding of Social Security for the future. What the U.S. Congress is doing is taking that $170 billion surplus from last year, a surplus of roughly $170 billion this year, and enormous projected surpluses over the coming decade, and spending it—and replacing it with government IOUs—known as U.S. Treasury notes.

One would think this has to change.

We need to change the legislation to allow for a legitimate investment of surplus funds into "high-quality" hard and financial assets. We should take these surplus funds and consider buying top-rated, marketable securities of all types—corporate bonds, domestic stocks, selected foreign securities, gold, commercial real estate, and so forth.

Then, in the future, when those Social Security funding pressures are enormous, the Social Security administrators can then go to the back room, pick out a couple of these assets, a couple of those, receipts for gold, deeds for commercial real estate, and the like. They can then take these legitimate hard and financial assets to global financial markets, sell them, and get something in exchange called *real money*.

Right now it's not happening.

MEDICARE AND MEDICAID

While anxiety regarding future spending on Social Security draws the majority of the public's attention, it is the Medicare program that is the most financially challenged. Federal spending on this program, which provides health insurance for people 65 and older as well as for younger disabled people, reached roughly $374 billion in FY2006, a 12 percent rise from FY2005.

$68 Trillion

The estimated $68 trillion unfunded liability of the Medicare program exceeds that of all other entitlement programs combined. The president's unnecessary prescription drug program enacted in early 2006 only made this problem worse.

The frightening surge in spending in these programs of recent years, combined with projections of sharply higher spending in coming decades, makes it crystal clear that changes will have to be made. As with other programs, the sooner changes are made, the better.

Modest-means testing in regards to Medicare premiums paid by program beneficiaries will become increasingly commonplace in coming years. No alternative to such a change seems viable. The imminent retirement of tens of millions of Baby Boomers simply mandates increasing utilization of income-based criteria for costs and benefits in all entitlement areas.

Medicaid

Federal spending on Medicaid now exceeds $300 billion annually, with an enormous near-matching contribution from the states. This program, which provides health insurance for the poor, has strapped many states with double-digit spending increases in recent years.

In fact, the surge in Medicaid funding by the states now finds the program as the largest and fastest growing of all state expenditures. In many states, spending on Medicaid now exceeds spending on elementary and secondary education.

The Medicaid program is somewhat unique as far as entitlement programs. The reason? The level of state spending on the program strongly influences the level of federal matching funds to the states. The net result is that benefit levels vary among the states.

Medicaid was expanded as a result of welfare reform a decade ago. The number of Medicaid recipients, now 54 million, exceeds the number of people (48 million) now receiving Social Security.

Budget Buster

Already excessive government spending will expand faster in coming years as a result of the poorly designed and enormously expensive Medicare prescription drug benefit program that began on January 1, 2006. Senior citizens around the country were bombarded with mailbox literature professing the value of one or another of nearly 40 alternative plans to choose from.

Projected costs have been political dynamite. When Congress debated the potential program in 2005, the projected cost was $400 billion over 10 years. That estimate quietly rose to more than $500 billion. Estimated costs continued to rise, with some estimates now exceeding $1 trillion over 10 years. Fortunately, total spending in the first year came in lower than expected.

The Bush administration and the former Republican congressional leadership thought the prescription drug program would engender them to the hearts of seniors for years to come. However, the complexity of the program will do no such thing. The unfunded liability of this program alone is now twice that of Social Security.

This unnecessary drug benefit program, pushed heavily by the administration in 2005, serves to weaken President Bush's hand in leading a bipartisan effort toward overall entitlement cost containment. Such an arduous but necessary task will perhaps fall to the next administration.

CHAPTER 5

INFLATION, MONEY,

— AND —

INTEREST RATES

INFLATION

Why have inflation pressures remained under control since the early 1990s? The short answer is the powerful rise in worker productivity and intense domestic and global competition in nearly every major industry.

Stable U.S. inflation pressures have been a positive development in recent years (see Figure 5.1). Economic theory—and U.S. economic history—has typically linked extended economic expansions and associated tight labor markets with inevitable surges in inflation pressures.

Under Wraps

Four primary reasons have kept U.S. inflation pressures at bay and will continue to do so in coming years:

First, there is an incredible amount of domestic and global competition in nearly every major industry in the world. An estimated one-third excess capacity exists in most major global industries, from automakers to steelmakers to computer makers to you-name-it makers.

In many cases, companies generally lack "pricing power"—the ability to raise prices and see those increases stick. In fact, thousands of companies are frequently forced to *cut* prices as a means of defending or obtaining market share.

Second, our behavior as American consumers has changed in recent years. Step back to the mid- to late 1970s. Inflation was getting worse each year. We walked into a store where we had an eye on a product. The price was higher than it was the week before.

What did we do then? We might have bought the product because we were fearful of what the price may be the following week or the following month. We don't do that anymore.

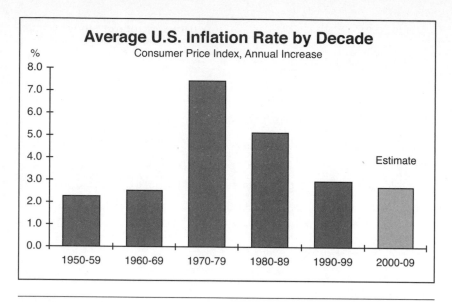

FIGURE 5.1 Average Inflation Rate by Decade

Source: Based on data from the U.S. Bureau of Labor Statistics.

Consumers today are bolder and more aggressive—and we are more willing to negotiate prices on more products than ever before. Many consumers say to the retailer, "This is my price. I can buy this product at Wal-Mart or another discounter at a better price. I can go to the Internet. If you cut your price, I will buy from you." This more aggressive attitude by consumers helps keep inflation in check.

The third reason is technology. U.S. corporations invested $2.5 trillion in technology during the 1990s and have made record annual investments in recent years. That investment is now paying substantial dividends. The result? Worker productivity rose 3.0 percent annually (on average) during 2002 through 2006, the strongest five-year gain in more than 40 years.

The fourth reason is the Internet. Various estimates suggest that global companies will save as much as $1.25 trillion in operating costs over the next three years by using the Internet.

Bond Power

In addition to the four factors just described, another powerful force will *demand* that inflation pressures remain under control. This force will focus on the monetary policy of the Federal Reserve and rebel quickly at even the slightest hint of irresponsible, and inflationary, policy changes. This force is the American bond market, described later in the section titled "The Dog and the Tail."

The PCE Index

One lesson learned by financial market participants since the mid-1980s was to pay attention to the economic "stuff" on which Federal Reserve officials focused. For example, nobody cared much about the quarterly Employment Cost Index until former Federal Reserve Chair Alan Greenspan noted that it was one of his favorite statistics.

Similarly, Greenspan was known to favor the U.S. Commerce Department's monthly measure of the Personal Consumption Expenditures (PCE) index as a better consumer inflation gauge than the U.S. Labor Department's Consumer Price Index (CPI). The Fed has now increasingly focused on the PCE core rate, which excludes volatile food and energy prices.

The PCE is regularly updated to reflect changes in consumer spending patterns and is also considered a more comprehensive measure of consumer prices. Federal Reserve officials have long complained that the CPI overstates inflation, in part because of its reliance on a somewhat static (slowly changing) basket of goods to be measured.

THE FEDERAL RESERVE

The Federal Reserve is easily one of the most powerful—and misunderstood—of all American institutions. The Federal Reserve's steady hand as America's "central banker" has been especially critical to U.S. economic performance during the past 25 years. Why?

The management of fiscal policy (taxation and spending) was less than admirable during the majority of those years by various presidential administrations and congresses. As a result, the enormous and irresponsible buildup of federal debt remains, for now, our collective lasting legacy.

Today's Federal Reserve—under the control of Chair Ben Bernanke—enjoys a very high level of credibility as an inflation fighter. In the world of central banks, there is no loftier objective... nor any greater success.

Inflation Control

The Federal Reserve's number one responsibility is to maintain American price stability. It has been largely successful over the past 15 years in doing so, with consumer prices rising at an average annual rate of 2.6 percent since 1991. More comprehensive measures of inflation have risen at even lesser rates. In contrast, U.S. consumer prices rose an average of 6.2 percent annually during the 1970s and 1980s, with a painful bout of double-digit inflation in 1979 and 1980.

Today's Fed is very concerned that higher energy prices impacting the economy will contribute to a broad series of price increases for thousands of products and services across the economy. Such a pass-through of energy costs keeps Fed officials awake at night.

Add in volatile commodity and gold prices, potential avian flu, the fear of further terrorism in the United States and abroad, enormous purchases of U.S. Treasury securities by foreign investors, and a handful of other topics, and one gets a feel for the life of a Fed official. It is not for the fainthearted.

In its efforts to maintain price stability, the Fed many times is called upon to:

1. "Take the punch bowl away from the party" (to slow the economy) when it gets a bit too rowdy.

2. Administer preventive "medicine" to its patient (the U.S. economy) when necessary in order to minimize the chance of a more serious "inflation disease" later, which would require even more drastic action (more painful medicine).

Note that most changes to monetary policy are enacted by the Fed adding reserves to or withdrawing reserves from the banking system through a process called *open market operations*. The result of such moves is to increase or decrease the Fed's most critical interest rate, the *federal funds rate*. The federal funds rate is the rate at which commercial banks and certain other financial institutions invest excess funds with other commercial banks on an overnight unsecured basis.

The federal funds rate is easily the most important of *all* short-term interest rates. Changes in the federal funds rate immediately impact the level of all other short-term interest rates, including the prime lending rate and various short-term investment rates. The discount rate, the other rate controlled by the Fed, is now almost irrelevant to the conduct of contemporary monetary policy.

The Dog and the Tail

While many of the Federal Reserve's official responsibilities remain unchanged from earlier years, the nature of the Federal Reserve's monetary policy flexibility has changed markedly during the past 30 years. In my opinion, the Federal Reserve is no longer the primary determinant of when monetary policy changes are necessary—the U.S. bond market is.

From the Federal Reserve's creation in 1913 until the late 1970s, the Federal Reserve solely determined monetary policy. The nation's bond market—much smaller during those times—quietly fell in line. During that era, the Federal Reserve was the "dog" while the bond market was the "tail." This relationship is now reversed.

Today's reality is that the Federal Reserve, to a large extent, provides the monetary policy mix that is demanded by a powerful and very inflation-sensitive bond market. The market is now the "dog," while the Federal Reserve is the "tail."

Today's inflation-wary bond market provides the Federal Reserve with less monetary policy flexibility than at any time in its history. Any future Federal Reserve attempt to overstimulate U.S. economic growth with "easy money" would be met with rising long-term interest rates (in order to protect lenders and investors from impending higher inflation) and cries of Federal Reserve irresponsibility. See Silver Bullet #3 later in this chapter.

Conducting Monetary Policy

How does the Federal Reserve determine proper monetary policy? The Fed is clearly concerned about the inflation implications of today's historically tight labor markets and the wage pressures that could result.

Figuratively speaking, today's Federal Reserve conducts monetary policy using an old-style balancing scale with four trays in which the Fed balances:

1. Criticism from the "hawks" who see inflation under every rock. The hawks are typically critical of the Fed, noting that the institution is not aggressive enough in diffusing inflationary expectations.

2. Criticism from the "doves" who constantly argue that monetary policy is too restrictive. The doves argue that the Fed has usually gone too far in monetary tightening or has not eased policy enough, and that the Fed frequently threatens the economy with the "r" word—recession.

3. Recent price performance of gold and various other commodities. Price movements in these commodities can serve as inflation red flags, as well as signs of monetary policy that is too restrictive.

4. The current shape and slope of the U.S. Treasury yield curve, including the most recent direction of 10-year U.S. Treasury note and 30-year U.S. Treasury bond yields. Such information provides a clue as to the bond market's collective view of inflation expectations.

Only when all trays are in "relative balance" does the Fed consider monetary policy to be appropriate.

The Fed must also consider the inflation implications of U.S. dollar strength or weakness relative to other global currencies. The Fed must also consider the conduct of monetary policy by other major central banks including the European Central Bank, the Bank of England, and the Bank of Japan.

Monetizing the Debt

A question I am frequently asked is, "Won't the Federal Reserve at some point be forced to 'monetize the debt'—that is, to buy huge additional amounts of U.S. Treasury securities with newly created money—and finally deal with the $9.0 trillion gross national debt?" My answer is always *no.*

Of all the things one can worry about in the "dismal science" of economics, that question is one over which I never lose any sleep. History, especially in certain Latin American and European countries, provides vivid illustrations of how central bank abuses of monetary policy have led to short or extended periods of hyperinflation.

Today, however, the powerful U.S. bond market—now the Federal Reserve's overseer—simply *will not* allow that "easy solution" to the deficit problem. The new "dog"—the bond market—is now firmly in control.

The Maestro

Alan Greenspan will enter the financial history books as one of the most highly regarded chairs of the Federal Reserve. His reign of just under 19 years was the second longest ever, from 1987 to early 2006, during which he served under four U.S. presidents.

Mr. Greenspan was at the monetary controls during the stock market crash of 1987; the 1990 to 1991 recession; the Asian financial crisis of 1998; the Long-Term Capital Management meltdown soon after; the recession of 2000 to 2001; the horrific events of September 11, 2001; and on board during most of the longest bull market in stocks in history. He also minded the store during one of history's most painful stock market corrections.

Mr. Greenspan did an outstanding job during his reign at the Federal Reserve. His stature and respect in the nation's capital was second to none. Greenspan took bold steps during his tenure to remove much of the Fed's operating mystique. His push toward greater openness and "transparency" was very favorable.

The New Kid

Prior to 2001, current Federal Reserve Chair Ben Bernanke was largely unknown in global financial circles and served as head of the economics department at Princeton University. He ultimately served as a member of the Federal Reserve Board from August 2002 to June 2005.

Bernanke rapidly became the second most influential person on that seven-member board. In June 2005, he was selected by President George W. Bush to serve as the chair of the President's Council of Economic Advisors, presumably in an effort to broaden his government experience. His nomination to lead the Federal Reserve followed in late 2005.

The learning curve of the Fed chair is a very difficult one and not for the faint of heart. Bernanke had the big shoes of Alan Greenspan to fill, just like Greenspan had a learning curve to fill the big shoes of Paul Volcker in the mid-1980s.

Many people initially questioned Bernanke's inflation-fighting resolve, a perception that needed to be reversed quickly. Fed Chair Ben Bernanke stumbled a few times in trying to get comfortable in what is arguably the second most important job on the planet. His every word drew intense scrutiny and analysis. Many of us in the "crystal ball gazing" community would argue that no other person in the American economy, including the president, has more day-to-day impact on our lives in the form of influencing inflation and interest rates.

The Speech

Every Fed chair is forced early in their reign to give what I call "the Speech." It is a no-holds-barred personal testament that the Fed under their leadership will keep inflation at low levels, even when such policy can upset politicians, consumers, and financial market players in the United States and around the world. While such resolve can clearly disappoint financial markets in the short run, such policy is the essential groundwork for sustained, noninflationary growth and higher stock and bond prices in coming years.

Bernanke has continued his predecessor's moves towards transparency. Earlier in his professional career he expressed support of "inflation targeting." This entails announcing a targeted annual range for inflation pressures (say 1 percent to 2 percent) and then modifying monetary policy as needed to stay within the range. This practice is closely followed by the European Central Bank.

Greenspan opposed inflation targeting, preferring the flexibility to modify monetary policy to meet his whims and those of the financial community. One policy is not necessarily better than the other.

Fed Chair Greenspan had a unique ability to *talk* a great deal and *say* very little. Greenspan's ability to construct lengthy sentences—packed with verbiage foreign to many—was legendary, leaving many listeners scratching their heads. In contrast, Bernanke's style is much more direct, with short responses to questions, using words and phrases with which we are more familiar.

The Next Chair

It was very clear to financial market players in 2005 that President Bush would nominate a new Federal Reserve chair from a select list of highly qualified people. Why? This country learned a painful lesson when Jimmy Carter was president in the late 1970s.

At that time, Carter decided not to reappoint powerful Arthur Burns as chair of the Federal Reserve. He opted instead to replace him with a monetary unknown named G. William Miller, then serving as chair of Textron Corporation.

The reaction on Wall Street and of the global financial community was one of utter disbelief. Miller knew little of monetary policy, was merely viewed as a Carter puppet, and suffered an enormous lack of credibility, particularly with bond and foreign exchange markets around the globe.

Timing is everything. Monetary policy credibility was a major necessity in the late 1970s as inflation and interest rates kept moving

> # SILVER BULLET #3: LOW LONG-TERM INTEREST RATES
>
> High levels of confidence in the Federal Reserve's ability to restrain inflation pressures exist today. Such confidence will continue as the nation's bond market—the Fed's overseer—will simply not allow any return of irresponsible Federal Reserve monetary policy.
>
> Such confidence will allow long-term interest rates to remain at low levels, benefiting both home buyers and others who seek funding in the credit markets. This issue is the third of four major developments, referred to as Silver Bullets, that drive my optimistic view of the American economy in coming years.

higher and higher, while the U.S. dollar was falling lower and lower. In essence, the emperor had no clothes.

President Carter was ultimately "forced" by financial markets to replace ineffective Fed Chair Miller with a highly regarded monetary expert, Paul Volcker, in order to right a ship listing badly. Such monetary history clearly suggests that when Bernanke ultimately steps down, he will be replaced by someone from a short list of men and women with whom financial markets would be entirely comfortable.

Credibility

The Federal Reserve is a most unique institution. It has the ability to create and destroy "money" at will. (This process has nothing to do with a printing press and a great deal to do with open market operations. See again the prior discussion in this chapter.) Such power is an awesome responsibility.

The Fed *must* have unquestioned credibility as an inflation fighter. The Fed under Chairs Burns and Miller (1970s) lost it…the Fed under Volcker gained it back…the Fed under Greenspan strengthened it…

Without that credibility, the Fed has nothing.

OTHER CENTRAL BANKS

The Federal Reserve, America's central bank, engaged in a significant monetary tightening program between June 2004 and June 2006. The Fed's intent was to "sop up" or remove the excess monetary stimulus that it dumped into the U.S. economy between early 2001 and June 2003. The Fed's intent at that time was threefold:

1. The Fed was concerned that the U.S. economic weakness emerging in late 2000 and in 2001 would escalate into something more painful and enduring.

2. The Fed was concerned about the emotional impact of September 11, 2001, on the American psyche in terms of overall economic activity.

3. The Fed was deeply concerned that the American economy could suffer the same deflationary pressures that had severely impacted Japan.

Ultimately, the Fed engineered 13 consecutive reductions in its key federal funds rate beginning in January 2001, pushing the rate to a 46-year low of 1.00 percent between June 2003 and June 2004.

Beginning in June 2004, the Fed, through its 12-member Open Market Committee (FOMC), began what we affectionately refer to as the water torture approach to monetary policy. The Fed enacted 17 consecutive 0.25 percent increases in the federal funds rate to a level of 5.25 percent in June 2006, a level that prevailed well into 2007.

Until fall 2005, the Fed was acting alone as far as the three major central banks within the global community are concerned—then all three were on center stage.

In Europe

The European Central Bank (ECB), which represents the 12 nations using the euro, began tightening monetary policy during fall 2005 with an increase from 2.00 percent to 2.25 percent in its key short-term interest rate. The ECB followed with a series of additional tightening moves in 2006 and 2007. The ECB chair suggested that additional moves could occur later, since inflation exceeded its "mandated" cap of 2 percent annually.

While America's Federal Reserve had been tightening in an environment of solid U.S. economic growth, such was not the case in Europe. The European economy was growing at a sluggish 1 percent to 2 percent annual pace after inflation. While sluggish by American standards, such growth approached the strongest in six years in the European community.

What compelled the ECB to restrict monetary growth and threaten the modest European economic growth pace? Quite simply, the ECB's mandate is much more focused on inflation containment than is that of the Federal Reserve.

The German history of hyperinflations following World Wars I and II strongly contributed to the strict inflation targets. The ECB is almost "forced" to tighten monetary policy if inflation exceeds 2 percent on an annual basis. The rise in energy prices of recent years has impacted the European price level as well as our own.

Such monetary tightening was not welcome by European political leaders who struggle with citizen anger over sluggish economic growth and high levels of unemployment. Many young people find limited opportunities to obtain quality jobs, especially in the "Old

Europe" of France, Germany, Italy, and Spain. A respite from high global oil prices would be a most welcome development in Europe as well as within the United States.

In Japan

In March 2006, the Bank of Japan, that nation's central bank, announced a departure from the "quantitative easing" monetary policy of the prior five years, a fancy name for essentially zero short-term interest rates.

The Dow at 2500

Picture the despondent and sickly nature of the U.S. economy if the Dow Jones Industrial Average, north of 12000 in late 2006 and early 2007, were to fall steadily and painfully towards the mid-2000s over the next 13 years. Millions of American citizens would see their investment portfolios nearly wiped out.

Consumer and corporate spending would dry up on the way down as American economic optimism of the past decade would be replaced with despondency and fear of what tomorrow may bring. Spending would nosedive, savings would rise, hundreds of thousands of workers would lose their jobs, and pessimism would be rampant. This accurately describes the Japanese economy since late 1989.

The Nikkei Index, the primary measure of Japanese stocks, topped out near 39500 in late 1989, during what turned out to be the peak of Japan's bubble economy. The index then headed south in an extremely painful and consistent way, bottoming out below 8000 in 2003's second quarter—a loss of nearly 80 percent, and a loss of trillions of investor dollars. Such a painful decline was similar to the Nasdaq's plunge earlier in this decade.

The Bank of Japan responded *slowly* with more aggressive moves to help stimulate the economy. Japan's political leadership also responded *slowly* with increasingly aggressive spending plans to help revive the economy. Along the way, Japan's leadership incurred the largest national debt (as it relates to the size of the economy) ever recorded by a major nation.

Incidentally, we have anxiety in the United States about the gross national debt of roughly $9 trillion in a $13.5 trillion annual economy. The U.S. national debt is roughly 67 percent the size of our economy. Japan's national debt is 150 percent the size of theirs!

Deflation

A laggard Japanese economy, a dismal stock market, and consumer pessimism eventually gave way to a period of deflation, or declining prices, beginning in 1997. This painful deflation, the first recorded by a major nation since the Great Depression, only added to the economic misery.

During a deflationary period, consumers and businesses have even less incentive to spend money. Spending is delayed in expectation of lower prices later. Business investment is curtailed because of expectations of declining sales. In addition, declining prices for goods and services, residential and commercial real estate, and other assets are eventually followed by declining wages.

Japanese economic output was $4.7 trillion in 2006, slightly larger than in 1990. In contrast, the U.S. economy grew from $6.6 trillion in output in 1990 to $13.5 trillion in 2006.

Just after the turn of the century (that still sounds funny), the Bank of Japan pulled out all the stops and flooded the economy with trillions of additional yen. The result was the nation's key short-term interest rate fell to near zero (actually 0.01 percent) in hopes of reigniting economic growth.

And, yes, some desired inflation.

Better News

Private-sector economic growth returned to Japan in 2004. Moderate growth over the past few years was more in line with that of the United States and Europe. The Nikkei doubled to 16000 by 2005 and near 18000 in early 2007. In addition, consumer prices rose slightly in 2006, following eight painful years of modest deflation.

Japan's central bank announced in March 2006 that it would discontinue its extremely aggressive monetary stimulus. It did point out, however (to help offset anxiety of politicians and business leaders), that short-term interest rates would remain extremely low for a considerable period of time. The Bank of Japan boosted its key rate by 0.25 percent in both mid-2006 and early 2007.

Japan's economy has been the global community's albatross for years, contributing almost nothing to global performance. As the globe's second largest economy, growth is critical. That growth is finally emerging.

A Dozen Plus

To the central banks of the United States, Europe, and Japan, one could also add central banks of the British and of the Canadians. Each engaged in tightening in recent years. In fact, central banks of more than a dozen different nations tightened monetary policy during summer 2006 in order to offset energy-induced inflation pressures, even as the Federal Reserve took a breather from additional tightening.

INTEREST RATES

The general public's basic misunderstanding of the role played by the Federal Reserve in the conduct of monetary policy continues. I frequently get asked, "Should I lock in my mortgage rate now in case the Fed raises mortgage rates in the next few months?"

Who Determines Short-Term Interest Rates?

The Federal Reserve is the sole determinant of the level of *short-term* interest rates in the U.S. economy. The federal funds rate, the rate at which commercial banks and other financial institutions lend excess funds to other commercial banks on an unsecured overnight basis, is the most important short-term interest rate of all. Every other short-term interest rate—including the prime lending rate, commercial paper, U.S. Treasury bills, and short-term bank certificates of deposit—is closely aligned with the Federal Reserve's federal funds rate.

The Federal Reserve has historically been associated with the discount rate. However, in today's financial world the discount rate has become largely irrelevant. If the Federal Reserve were to announce tomorrow that it was discontinuing use of the discount rate, nobody would care. The conduct of open market operations—which focus on the federal funds rate—is now front and center.

Who Determines Long-Term Interest Rates?

Long-term interest rates are determined by the "market"—individuals and institutional buyers and sellers of long-term fixed-rate U.S. Treasury, corporate, mortgage-backed, foreign, "junk" (excuse me, *high-yield*), and tax-exempt bonds. Just as buyers and sellers determine the price of IBM or Intel stock, or the value of the U.S. dollar in global financial markets, so do market participants determine the price (and corresponding yield or return) of long-term, fixed-income securities and mortgages.

Mortgage rates are indirectly tied to the yield on 10-year U.S. Treasury notes. The traditional rule of thumb has been to take the 10-year U.S. Treasury note yield and add 1.5 percent to 1.6 percent in order to roughly determine the current rate on 30-year fixed-rate mortgages.

At the same time, the 10-year U.S. Treasury note has largely replaced the 30-year U.S. Treasury bond as the key benchmark long-term security. This change is in line with the norm around the global marketplace.

Inversion

An unusual interest rate development occasionally draws serious attention within the financial community, as it did during much of 2006 and at times in 2007, that is, an inversion of the yield curve (which sounds like something from *Star Trek*). The typical invest-ment "rule" is the longer the investment period, the higher the inter-est rate or return. This is very much a commonsense relationship. This relationship is known as a *positive yield curve.*

For example, an investor in bonds would typically be rewarded with a higher interest rate to invest for 10 years versus 2 years. The logic is the same for a depositor in a financial institution being offered a higher interest rate for a longer-dated certificate of deposit.

An Inversion History

At times, however, the interest rate, or yield, on short-term bonds actually exceeds the rate, or yield, on longer-maturity bonds. This can occur when the Federal Reserve is pushing short-term inter-est rates sharply higher to fend off inflation, such as when the Fed pushed its key federal funds rate as high as 19 percent in the early 1980s. At that time, the yield on 2-year U.S. Treasury notes was near 17.00 percent, while the return on 10-year U.S. Treasury notes was around 15.75 percent. A serious recession soon followed.

We experienced another inversion a few years ago, with yields on both 2-year and 10-year U.S. Treasury Notes around 8.00 percent.

An inversion also occurred during much of 2006, with both 2-year and 10-year U.S. Treasury yields around 4.75 percent to 5.00 percent.

A Recession Signal?

Various bond market historians point out that such an inversion in yields is always a precursor of recession. Current inversion-means-recession skeptics, including me, see things differently. Even former Federal Reserve Chair Greenspan suggested that the relationship between inversions and pending recessions was less direct.

In the most current case, the level of interest rates is historically low. Following 17 monetary tightening moves by the Fed since June 2004, the federal funds rate reached 5.25 percent in 2006's second quarter.

Long-term interest rates were also remarkably low, especially given the inflation anxiety that gripped financial markets in 2006. Ten-year U.S. Treasury note yields ranged between 4.50 percent and 5.30 percent during most of 2006. Investment yields were only marginally above the level of long-term interest rates two years before, when the federal funds rate was at a 46-year low of 1.00 percent from June 2003 to June 2004.

Why did long-term interest rates not move sharply higher, reacting to the sharp rise in short-term interest rates and higher U.S. inflation? Two reasons come to mind.

The first was the enormous global flow of funds into U.S. Treasury securities. The Chinese, Japanese, Saudis, and other nations enjoyed enormous revenue from huge trade surpluses and high oil prices.

What to do with the money? Tens of billions of dollars monthly soon found their way into U.S. Treasury securities, which are still the safest and most marketable investment on the planet. Such demand for Treasury securities kept long-term bond prices high—and yields low.

In addition, the Fed enjoys solid financial market credibility under Chair Bernanke as it did during Greenspan's tenure. Global investors are comfortable holding fixed-rate, longer-dated bonds because their confidence in the Fed's inflation control mentality is extremely high.

The fact that the Fed was willing to push short-term interest rates higher would, over time, increase the cost of using credit and lead to U.S. economic slowing. Economic slowing is typically associated with a lessening of inflationary pressures. This is the primary reason for greater investor comfort in holding fixed-income securities including long-term bonds.

The Fed's well-telegraphed moves to slow money creation and deal with inflation pressures was good news to long-term lenders and investors because future inflation was less likely to ravage their portfolios. The old adage of taking regular doses of distasteful medicine now to lessen the need for surgery later was appropriate.

GOLD

An attendee at one of my 2005 speaking engagements asked me where gold prices were headed. Given the upward momentum in gold prices at that time, I told him $500 per ounce seemed likely. I also told him that I would rather be a seller than a buyer at that price.

Whoops!

Gold prices, as well as prices of other major commodities, including silver, copper, and oil, continued to climb for awhile, defying the skeptics. Gold prices briefly exceeded $700 per ounce in mid-2006, reaching a 25-year high, before receding to lower levels.

Good news? Gold prices are high versus where they have been in recent years. "Gold bugs," those companies and salespeople who *always* recommend gold as the best investment in a scary world, *always* talk of gold going to higher and higher levels. They have finally been more accurate over the past few years as gold prices have more than doubled—even a broken clock is right twice a day.

Bad news? Gold is arguably the single *worst* investment of the past 26 years. Gold prices today would have to be around $1,975 per ounce to equal (in purchasing power) the peak price of gold in January 1981 of around $847 per ounce.

A Safe Haven

Why have gold prices risen? The traditional argument is that gold represents "a safe haven" for investors when the global community is crazier, or riskier, than usual. Given the recent combination of global terrorism, war in Iraq, nuclear ambitions in Iran and North Korea, potential and real oil supply disruptions in various markets, the risk of an avian flu pandemic, and other issues, a valid case can be made to diversify investment holdings.

As a matter of fact, portfolio diversification has *always* been a good idea.

Add in bad behavior by too many corporate executives, concerns about global inflation, and concerns about a global flight away from dollar-denominated assets, and the gold advocates have been in seventh heaven.

Don't Hold Your Breath

At this writing, I am currently holding a full-page newspaper ad that has been multiplying like rabbits. It is everywhere! This ad, as well as many others like it, speaks of gold prices moving higher. The ad quotes the "experts" by noting "the explosive upside potential of reaching up to $2,000 an ounce." In another paragraph, the ad reads: "As predicted, the Gold Market is well on its way towards the $2,000 an oz. mark." It strongly recommends the purchase from them of special gold coins now, which are, conveniently, available for the first time in history!

Ownership of gold is somewhat unique and shares its peculiarity with diamonds. Whereas most other commodities, such as steel, copper, wheat, and soybeans, are produced to ultimately be consumed or used, gold is held by millions of people around the world for its beauty and presumed retention of value.

There is little doubt that aggressive investors pushed American stock prices higher in the late 1990s. Many of these investors then shifted their funds to American real estate (especially on both coasts and in the Southwest during the past five years). Many have since become part of the investor group pushing gold prices higher.

From Here?

I can't give you a solid forecast as to where gold prices are going. I am *not* a believer that U.S. budget deficits and U.S. trade imbalances will cause a global dumping of the dollar, pushing inflation pressures sharply higher, along with sharply higher gold prices.

I can, however, provide one solid piece of investment advice that I have used regularly in writing and speaking during the past 36 months in regard to rising American real estate values:

Bulls and bears can make money.

Pigs get slaughtered.

So be careful.

CHAPTER 6

—THE CONSUMER—

CONSUMER INCOMES

There is a saying that one can drown in a river that *averages* only six inches deep. Nowhere else in the American economy is data selectively twisted and tortured more than to support a political point of view regarding growth in real incomes in recent years.

Democrats massage the data to note that real incomes have not risen at all over select time periods, but continue to deteriorate. Hence, Republican policies are hurting millions of American families.

Republicans play the same numbers game. They select income data and time periods to support their view that Republican policies are helping the majority of American families. Both sides roll out fancy reports interpreted by highly esteemed academics or think tank experts, each side trying to outdo the other.

One thing is clear. The tighter U.S. labor market of the past 24 months has led to rising worker incomes in both nominal and real terms. Growth in total compensation during 2006 was the strongest in nearly a decade. In fact, recent income gains that outpaced the rise in worker productivity have again raised the specter of inflation.

Anemic growth in the American labor force over the next two decades in what is already a near-full employment economy will continue to enhance the real income gains of a majority of workers. This reality is one that drives my optimistic view of the American economy and the ability of a majority of American workers to prosper in coming years.

Poverty

The share of Americans living in poverty was estimated at 12.6 percent in 2005. This includes people living below the poverty line, or an income of about $20,000 for a family of four. This rate has stayed stubbornly high for decades. This data does not include the value of food stamps, welfare payments, school lunch programs, Medicaid, housing assistance, or the earned income tax credit, all of which are geared to enhance standards of living for lower-income families.

Shifting Quintiles

Significant political discussion has taken place in recent years about earnings growth in the various income strata—typically divided into fifths or quintiles. Much of the political rhetoric suggests that "the rich get richer, while the poor get poorer." The assumption is also made that people tend to stay in the same income quintiles for years with little movement between income groups.

This assumption is dead wrong.

Research from various studies has noted the tremendous changes that occur as people move between the various income groups. Reasons for these shifts include retirement, beginning or ending college attendance and employment training programs, moving from part-time to full-time work, moving from full-time to part-time employment, extended illness, lengthy periods of unemployment, and numerous other factors.

Dual-Income Households

Millions of American families with small children struggle with the issues related to two working spouses. While one spouse may desire to stay home and be directly involved in raising children, the perceived need for additional income may require both spouses to work full-time (see Table 6.1).

One often overlooked factor in the decision to have both husband and wife work full-time is the additional expenses generated. A thorough cost-benefit analysis can often yield surprising results.

With two young kids, a couple's budget might look like this:	
Dual income	**$100,000**
Less payroll taxes of 23%	−23,000
Net take-home pay	77,000
Child care	−15,000
Extra transportation	−4,800
Dining out	−4,600
Extra work clothes & dry cleaning	−2,500
House cleaning	−2,600
Adjusted net income	**$47,500**
One income with two young kids	**$60,000**
Less payroll taxes of 18%	−10,800
Net income	**$49,200**

TABLE 6.1   Is It Worth It?

Source: Thredgold Economic Associates.

When one considers additional expenses such as costly child care (especially on both coasts), additional clothing and accessories, more takeout meals and restaurant dining, dry cleaning, a possible home cleaning service, extra transportation costs, higher taxes, as well as other possible costs, the differential between the net after-tax income of a dual-income household and a single-income household can be surprisingly minimal. In some cases, a dual-income household may even end up with less available income than the household with one breadwinner, as shown in Table 6.1.

After recognizing the modest increase in net after-tax income in many cases, the other considerations involve the emotional well-being of both the children and the stay-at-home spouse. Many children thrive in high-quality child care facilities, while other kids are miserable.

Many adults desire to stay at home and raise their children. Others need the social interaction and sense of accomplishment associated with working outside of the home. The answer? Decide what is best for your family, recognizing that additional income earned in most cases cannot be the primary reason for working.

CONSUMER SPENDING...
CONSUMER DEBT

The primary contributor to strong U.S. economic growth of recent years has been the American consumer. While the media typically focuses on the Dells, the Googles, the Fords, and the GEs of the world, the American economy is first and foremost a consumer economy, with consumer spending accounting for two-thirds of all U.S. economic performance.

A confident U.S. consumer—supported by strong job creation, restrained inflation, rising home equity, and higher incomes—spends money more aggressively, contributing to solid gains in retail sales and profitability. Conversely, an American consumer anxious about global terrorism, gyrating U.S. stock prices, corporate or political scandal, and job cuts spends money more cautiously, contributing to slack growth, or actual declines, in corporate performance.

Debt Burden

Americans traditionally shied away from debt—at least until the past 25 to 30 years. Easy access to credit of all types has now led to the highest level of U.S. consumer debt burdens on record.

Total consumer debt outstanding (excluding loans secured by real estate) first crossed the $1 trillion threshold in 1994 according to data collected by the Federal Reserve. Total consumer debt outstanding reached nearly $2.5 trillion in late 2006. At the same time, however, additional Federal Reserve data indicated that the net worth of the American household—the difference between total household assets and total household liabilities—exceeded $55 trillion at year-end 2006, three times the total of 18 years before.

The financial services industry has all shapes and sizes of lenders. These include both traditional players such as commercial banks and credit unions, as well as a whole new breed of lenders.

Those Credit Cards

The easiest ways to increase lender market share are to offer large lines of credit, attractive "teaser" rates, and to make loans to those formerly viewed as poor credit risks. Perhaps nowhere is this development more apparent than in credit card issuance and usage.

Aggressive lenders have flooded the market with preapproved lines of credit with extremely low teaser rates such as 5.9 percent, 2.9 percent, or even 0 percent for the first 3 to 12 months. The cost of such credit then quietly jumps to 15.9 percent, or 18.9 percent, or even higher at the end of the teaser period. Many consumers are then able to switch to another low-interest-rate card, while others are then buried in high-cost credit card debt.

Credit card solicitations are arguably the most common piece of "snail mail" that arrives daily for the typical American consumer. Millions of Americans have taken on higher levels of credit card debt.

Others, however, utilize credit cards for purchases of all types in order to generate frequent flier miles or points. Most of these users are then able to pay off the balance at the end of the month. These card users clearly distort historical comparisons of debt loads.

Tapping Home Equity

Millions of American homeowners have tapped into the rising equity in their homes in recent years. Financial institutions have made it easy to simply write a check against an approved line of credit in order to enjoy the rising equity.

Millions of responsible homeowners have tapped these home equity loans to pay off higher interest rate credit cards and other loans. Millions of others have tapped the equity to finance new home furnishings, exotic trips, new cars, swimming pools, and other expenditures.

Mortgage Debt

Another area of concern regarding consumer debt obligations is that used to purchase or refinance homes. During the past five years, millions of homeowners refinanced their existing home mortgages to take advantage of 40-year lows in mortgage interest rates, or as an opportunity to borrow more, or both. Many of these individuals improved their cash flow for years to come.

Many of these homeowners, as well as a large share of new home buyers, were required to use adjustable-rate or interest-only mortgages in order to qualify for the loans. Unfortunately, the combination of higher short-term interest rates and stagnant or declining home values on both coasts has created significant financial stress for many Americans, particularly those who entered transactions in 2006.

Better Shape

Despite the challenges noted above, the majority of Americans are in better overall financial condition than a generation ago. A near-full-employment U.S. economy, higher stock prices, solid gains in home values between 2000 and mid-2006, and moderate growth in real incomes of the past decade have helped tens of millions of Americans.

HOUSING

Financial markets of all types have always been prone to excess. The human experience leads us in that direction. I served as an adjunct professor of finance (teaching in the evening) at the University of

Utah from 1982 until 2000. I taught those close to graduation about "the real world" of the economy, the Federal Reserve, financial markets, job creation, inflation, and the like.

I used to tell my students that despite the near instantaneous flow of information around the world that was/is available today, financial market performance, especially in the near term, still came down to two base human emotions: fear and greed.

Nasdaq Excess

A simple history of the past six to seven years highlights investor excesses within the stock market. The Nasdaq (the acronym of the National Association of Securities Dealers Automated Quotations) was a great example of excessive greed. The Nasdaq peaked at 5049 in 2000's first quarter. As fear eventually took control, the Nasdaq plunged nearly 80 percent during the next 31 months to 1113, before its labored rise back north of 2500.

Similar behavior in emerging nation stock markets has occurred over the past few years, with spectacular increases followed by harrowing dives. The rise of oil, gold, and copper also, to an extent, reflect greed-driven markets.

Housing was another prime example. Solid U.S. economic growth of the past few years, combined with a rising population, low mortgage rates, and a lack of buildable land in many coastal markets did legitimately lead home prices higher.

Aggressive Investors

Another major factor? Where was the aggressive investment money in the U.S. economy in the second half of the 1990s? It was in the stock market, with tens of billions parked in Internet and other technology stocks.

Where did that aggressive investment money go during the 2000 to 2006 period as investors quickly soured of stock market pain? Tens of billions of dollars soon found their way into residential real estate, primarily on both coasts.

Legitimate buyers and speculators drove coastal and southwestern home prices higher, with many markets seeing prices double between 2001 and 2006. At the same time, however, average home values across the nation rose by roughly one-half.

Flippers

As coastal home prices moved higher and higher, many housing speculators soon relocated to markets in Arizona and Nevada, as well as smaller communities in California and Florida. The typical developer's mind-set was also too optimistic—"My new development will make me lots of money. It's the other builders who need to cut back."

Thousands of speculators bid up prices in new housing developments hundreds or thousands of miles from "home" with no intention of ever occupying the home or condo. Thousands of these "flippers" are now buried in costly properties and they face rising mortgage rates and weakening values. Thousands of properties will ultimately be foreclosed on by overly aggressive lenders who also got caught up in the game, particularly lenders in the subprime market.

The greed was too long in control.

Tens of thousands of homes and condos were also bought as second homes and/or retirement properties by Baby Boomers. Many of these properties have been or might be available for sale at an acceptable price. However, thousands of these properties will remain in Boomer portfolios for retirement use in coming years.

The national media's fixation on all things negative would almost have you believe that the bottom has simply fallen out of the American housing market. This is not the case.

New home sales and existing home sales were clearly weaker in 2006 and early 2007 than was the case in prior years. However, combined sales in 2006 still ranked as the third best year on record!

Reasonable Values

Many coastal states and communities are dealing with problems of prior excess. However, residents of many inland states and communities that largely missed the coastal excesses of the past few years are now enjoying their own housing renaissance.

Housing markets in the Rocky Mountain states, parts of the Midwest, parts of the Southwest, and the deep South did extremely well in 2006 and early 2007. Homes at logical and affordable prices are readily available.

While many speculators will have their heads handed to them in various markets, the average homeowner will be just fine. Bear in mind that the typical home seller is not a home flipper, but has been in their respective home for a number of years. While they may feel the pain of selling in a softer market, in many cases they have enjoyed sizable appreciation in prior years.

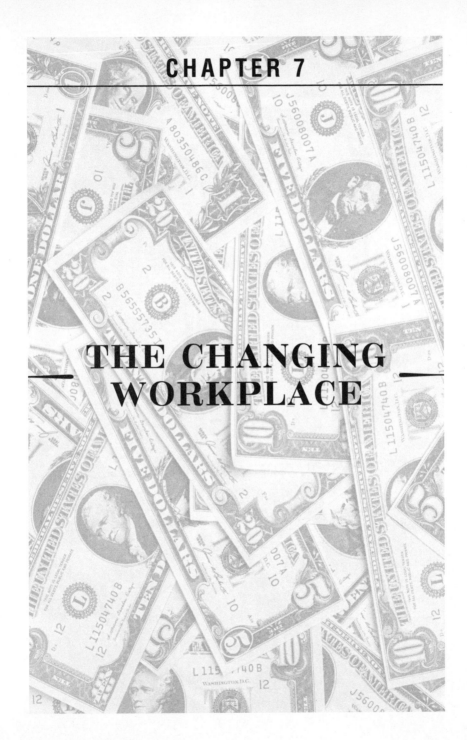

CHAPTER 7

THE CHANGING WORKPLACE

DEMOGRAPHICS

Longer life spans in the United States and around the world provide the opportunity for, and the challenge of, different age groups rubbing elbows in the workplace more than ever before. These generational interactions can be most interesting, with older people not always comfortable with how younger people think and act—and vice versa.

Four Major Demographic Groups

The Silent or Greatest Generation

The "Silents" are those Americans born between 1900 and 1945, with current ages of 62 and above. This group, exceeding 72 million strong, controls the vast majority of American wealth.

The Silents were primarily impacted by two world wars, the Great Depression, the automobile, and radio. This major group has experienced more in the way of good times and bad times than any subsequent group. It is also because of the sacrifices of the Greatest Generation in times of global war that younger groups have enjoyed the peace, prosperity, and limitless opportunities we now take for granted.

Millions of workers of this generation prided themselves in staying with one major employer for decades when the notion of lifetime employment was more available and accepted. Today's youngest workers look at such relationships in near disbelief.

Those between ages 65 and 69, should they choose to work, are able to take advantage of Social Security income rule changes enacted in 2000 that formerly reduced Social Security payments if earnings exceeded $17,000 annually. Those ages 70 and above were already free of these prior income limitations.

Don't be surprised to see such flexibility made available to workers between ages 62 and 64 in coming years. Each of these older age groups will become increasingly important as flexible and/or part-time workers in an American economy in desperate need of additional bodies.

Most Silents are now retired, although millions prefer to keep one foot in the workplace. American stock market weakness of 2000 to 2002 forced many formerly considering retirement to stay in the workplace longer. More recent stock market gains have allowed millions to enjoy active retirements.

The Baby Boom Generation

The Boomers are those Americans born between 1946 and 1964, with current ages between 43 and 61 years. This group, 78 million strong, has greatly impacted everything as we have aged, including the enormous surge of new entrants into elementary schools in the 1950s and 1960s; the subsequent move into secondary schools, colleges, and universities; the first-time home buyers' market; and the workplace. The Boomers imminent impact upon retirement will be no less powerful.

The Boomers were primarily shaped by the war in Vietnam, Watergate, and television. Boomers are the most well-educated generational group ever.

By various estimates, the Boomers will inherit $12 to $20 trillion from their parents in coming years, the largest generational wealth shift ever. I would suggest such a wealth shift from our parents will be dwarfed by what we leave our children and grandchildren.

At the same time, Boomers are frequently referred to as the "sandwich" generation. A significant share currently or will soon find themselves providing financial assistance to their parents at the same time they support their own children in expensive colleges and universities.

Despite a generation of denial, Boomers are subject to the reality of aging. References to one more Boomer reaching age 50 every seven seconds have been frequent in recent years. We now talk of one Boomer reaching the age of 60 every eight seconds, with the oldest Boomers eligible to draw Social Security in 2008 at age 62, with eligibility to qualify for Medicare three years later.

As they get older, Boomers will redefine the view of our golden years, with millions preferring to slowly bridge towards retirement, in other words, move from full-time work to perhaps working two or three days per week. Others will value workplace flexibility that might include, for example, two weeks on the job with two weeks off.

Millions of Boomers will never retire, but they will continue to do what they do well on their own desired schedules. Extraordinarily tight U.S. labor markets will be conducive to this desire. Enlightened American employers, who perceive such tight labor realities in coming years, will embrace these flextime concepts as a means of preserving access to valuable worker experience. Many employers who ignore such a future will struggle or simply cease to exist.

Generation X

These younger people are those born between 1965 and 1980, with current ages between 27 and 42 years. This group, roughly 55 million strong, is also known as the "Baby Bust Generation." They are the smallest of the four demographic groups.

The "Gen Xers" or simply "Xers" were primarily impacted by technology, television, day care, divorce, downsizing, and the events of September 11, 2001. They are independent, confident, skeptical, talented, and largely impatient with the status quo. They are now somewhat overlooked as the much larger "Generation Y" group is now entering their adult years.

While older workers prided themselves on spending 15 or 25 (or more) years with one employer, the Xers question why. They view this employment longevity as a weakness. The Xers see employment stability and security in mobility and constantly updated technological skills, with many preferring contract work and project assignments. They thrive when viewing themselves as entrepreneurs and need constant feedback.

This group has been much more comfortable with technology than have their parents and grandparents. The reason? The use of computers and other forms of technology has been part of their collective lives from the beginning.

Generation Y

This youngest of all generations includes those born between 1981 and today, with current ages between birth and 26 years. This group slightly exceeds the Boomers in size, with roughly 80 million members. Members of Generation Y are also referred to as the "Echo Boomers" and "Tidal Wave II." A professional speaker friend of mine trademarked the phrase "Generation Why," which certainly applies to this enormous group.

The Ys have been shaped by affluence, divorce, downsizing, September 11, and the explosion in personal technology. They are largely cut from the same cloth as their Boomer parents and grandparents, but are even more selective (and perhaps spoiled) than their predecessors.

Their large number is tied as much to rising foreign immigration as to the domestic birth rate. They represent a record school-age population, with substantial stress on all educational establishments.

The Ys have and will enter the workplace entirely comfortable with computers and technology of all types. These kids have been bombarded with information from an early age and have, in the opinion of many, grown up too rapidly.

The Ys were the first major generation to truly embrace the concept of multitasking, the reality of doing three or four things simultaneously. While this development took root with the prior generation, Generation Y has since taken this reality to a new art form. As parents and grandparents, we watch in near disbelief, for example, as the Ys do their homework, while "texting" their friends, while listening to their iPods, while watching television.

This generation already shares the distaste of their older brothers and sisters for lengthy engagements with one major employer, also preferring the stimulation and challenges of ever-changing employment situations. (Note to employers: Keep your Generation Y employees stimulated and challenged, with their perception that they are in charge of themselves, or watch them leave quickly for greener pastures.)

EDUCATION

One of the few no-brainers in the American economy today is the high value of education. An increasingly sophisticated economy demands that successful workers in nearly all employment sectors have the initial education/training to comprehend what is expected of them, as well as the ability to "learn as they go" on the job.

The disparity between the education "haves" and "have nots" will likely continue to widen as rising sophistication of the American and global economies continues to develop. Workers without adequate education are equivalent to boxers with one arm tied behind their backs.

The $$

Various measures of income suggest that college graduates make between 75 percent and 100 percent more than high school graduates. Such a relationship 25 years ago was closer to a 25 percent differential. Earnings of those with advanced degrees are even higher.

Each year of post–high school education of any type enhances lifetime earnings by an estimated 15 percent to 20 percent, according to various estimates. The economic evolution under way also rewards technical skills as never before.

Computer skills are obviously important, and are rewarded by the marketplace. The data suggests that if you have two people working in the same office with the same job description, with one person having good computer skills versus the other who lacks them, the person with solid computer skills earns as much as 15 percent to 20 percent more money. Traditional blue collar occupations also demand increasing technical skills as more physical or routine tasks are now performed by computerized machines and robotics guided by highly trained technicians.

The Education-Employment Connection

As one would expect, higher levels of educational attainment are closely connected to higher levels of employment in an increasingly sophisticated American economy and vice versa. The jobless rate for those with less than a high school diploma was 5.8 percent in early 2007.

In contrast, the jobless rate for high school graduates (with no college credit) was 4.2 percent. The jobless rate for workers with some college or an associate's degree was near 3.5 percent in early 2007, while the jobless rate for those with a bachelor's degree was below 2 percent.

The Old Days

The correlation between higher levels of educational attainment and higher incomes was not always so clear. The first 60 years of the 20th century was a period when physical strength was as important as mental agility in many industries, including most within the manufacturing sector.

Extraordinary productivity gains in the manufacturing sector, combined with the powerful rise of the Information Age, have changed this prior dynamic forever. Contrary to information pushed by the liberal national media, U.S. manufacturing has not declined. This nation produces more goods each year than before.

The difference is in regard to the number of people utilized in the manufacturing process. The greater use of automation, robotics, and powerful software has created the need for fewer workers even as manufacturing output climbs. This trend will only continue.

More and More

Educational attainment of Americans has grown sharply over the past century. A hundred years ago, few workers were high school graduates, while fewer still had attended or graduated from college. Most workers found jobs early in life out of a necessity to assist with family expenses or to work full time on family farms. One could argue that the enormous rise in educational attainment of the average American combines with the sharp rise in the average American life span as two of the most powerful developments of the past 100 years.

Then and Now

Workers in the nation's "blue collar" manufacturing sector were perhaps the most vulnerable to jobs lost to lower-production-cost locations over the past 25 years. Jobs lost to Mexico and more recently to China and other low-cost Asian nations have been painful for tens of thousands of American workers.

More recently, job losses among higher-educated people became center stage. The loss of white collar jobs to India of recent years has been significant, with many of these jobs in architecture, engineering, financial services, and research of all types.

Not Ready for Prime Time

Critics of American primary and secondary schools decry the poor educational skills of many young people leaving high schools today. Too many of these graduates simply do not possess the workplace skills of grammar, mathematics, and social interaction that contribute to being effective workers from the get-go.

Various education advocates clamor for greater educational funding, while others argue that a lack of teacher and administrative accountability is the problem. These critics suggest that the two major national teacher unions stifle accountability of teachers and limit competition between educational styles. There is plenty of blame to go around.

There is little argument that tens of thousands of young people leave public schools in the nation's inner cities and rural communities with severely limited skills to compete. Too many companies are forced to provide remedial instruction for new workers. This shortfall in the educational output in our inner cities is perhaps America's greatest educational shortcoming.

One positive development of recent years has been the willingness within select states and communities to experiment with education, including specialized (magnet) schools and charter schools. Parents around the country are taking a more proactive roll in examining the education process of their children, with particular interest from parents and guardians of youth in America's inner cities. Vouchers must be given greater consideration and testing. The rising value of preschool education in helping young children develop a solid foundation for future learning must also draw additional study.

A Tough Profession

Little doubt exists that the life of a public school educator within K through 12 grades is challenging. While attempting to educate children in basic skills, teachers are many times also required to address the demands of special and bilingual education, cultural awareness, and environmental education.

Many teachers find themselves discussing teen pregnancy, the avoidance of gang life and violence, the evils of tobacco and drugs, sex education, computer training, and helping kids develop social skills to interact well with others. Amy, my oldest daughter, has taught third grade in an inner-city school for 12 years. She would agree that each of the topics listed here, as well as many more, are a routine part of her challenging day. Things have certainly changed since I was in the K through 12 environment, when the four major issues were chewing gum, running in the halls, truancy, and spit wads.

The Community College Connection

Numerous communities around the nation have enjoyed major successes by putting local employers and educators in the same room to discuss and define the skills necessary for new labor force entrants to be successful.

What a concept!

The nation's community colleges and trade schools have seen their roles expand as the critical liaison between employers and students. As the American labor force becomes tighter and tighter, this community college/trade school role of matchmaker will become even more crucial.

Another View

The role of education is not simply to teach numbers, relationships, and theories to be regurgitated in testing environments. Today's most effective high schools, colleges, universities and other purveyors of education help their students learn *how* to learn, which is something quite different.

Much of today's educational reform efforts are focused on the notion of making young people more technology literate. Proponents desire to have up-to-date computers available to all students in all grade levels, suggesting that technical skills will be the defining element for future success or failure of our youth.

I would suggest that young people in coming years will find technology and computers so "user friendly" that the key to individual success will instead be traditional basic skills of reading, writing, communication, and social interaction. As a result, our education system needs to focus on the 4 Rs of readin', 'ritin', 'rithmetic, and relationships more than ever before.

Higher Education

One challenge for America is that much of the world is chasing—and catching—the United States as far as educational attainment. While older working Americans still lead the world in average educational attainment, many younger workers around the world are matching or exceeding the education levels attained by American workers.

One of America's strengths is the quality and diversity of our higher-learning institutions. American universities compete for students, professors, funding, research grants, and even athletes and musicians. As a result, high-profile institutions must constantly redefine their message and ensure their relevance.

American universities have also nurtured powerful connections between their institutions and the business world, with American universities earning substantial licensing fees and royalties each year. A rising number of state legislatures around the nation now routinely provide "seed money" to universities to develop and enhance such relationships.

One of America's higher-education strengths is a lack of central control over these institutions, with most university funding having limited connection to taxes. This reality contrasts with the European system where governments provide a majority of funding, and then demand excessive influence regarding programs.

This is another example of failed European central planning and control.

A Path

As noted previously, I served as an adjunct professor of finance at the University of Utah for 17 years, teaching upper-division classes in the evening. I would provide my students with two key views.

The first was that a future employer really did not care what the student learned in my class or any other class. Gaining a degree from an accredited college or university said something about one's intelligence and maturity. A degree "got you in the door," where the employer would teach the student what the employer wanted them to know, and how to best use the information.

Second, I would suggest to my students that their careers would likely follow paths much different than they expected. I suggested that many of these students would end up in occupations that had little, if anything, to do with their undergraduate training.

I used myself as an example. My undergraduate degree is in business administration. I was required to take three economics classes and liked none of them.

It was not until I had spent a number of years in the real world of bank portfolio management that economics became interesting. It was also at that time that my commercial banking superiors told me I was going back to school. They said I was evolving into an economist, but needed the academic training. I have now *worked* as an economist for the past 30 years or so.

With the term *worked* used loosely.

IMMIGRATION

The highly charged emotion regarding the issue of immigration into the United States is one that will not be going away anytime soon. An adequate exploration of immigration requires additional breakdown as to the legal and illegal aspects of the issue.

Legal Immigration

There is only limited debate as to the desirability of allowing thousands of legal immigrants into the United States annually. Many of these legal immigrants fill critical jobs within highly technical industries, strengthening America's role of being competitive in the world. Others are allowed into the United States because of political developments in their respective countries that could threaten their lives if they were forced to return to their homes.

A highly competitive global marketplace requires that American companies have access to the best and brightest around the world. Tens of thousands of American jobs have resulted from highly skilled and intelligent foreigners being allowed access to this country to live and work.

Nowhere is this fact more relevant than in the nation's technology sector, where many great American companies were founded or strengthened by attracting skilled foreign nationals to relocate to America. Many of these highly talented people have ultimately gained American citizenship.

One unfortunate development—resulting from the terrorist attacks of September 11, 2001—was a move by the U.S. Congress to severely restrict the flow of foreign nationals into the United States. Immigration quotas were tightened too much, with many companies frustrated in their attempts to attract global talent. Many foreign nationals who had been attending American universities also found their ability to stay in or gain access to the United States denied.

One detrimental result of such legal immigration overkill has been to push highly skilled people away from this nation. The subsequent homes established in other countries benefit companies in those nations. It is our collective loss.

American corporate leaders have had frequent discussions with their congressional representatives about the harm being done to their companies. It is in America's best interest for the Congress to increase the legal flow of talented immigrants to the United States. Fortunately, some progress is finally being made.

Illegal Immigration

The enormous flow of illegal immigrants (or *illegal aliens* as some prefer to describe them) into this country has emerged as a hot-button issue in recent years. This issue promises to be front and center as the 2008 election cycle approaches.

There are numerous proposals as to how to limit the flow of additional illegal immigrants to this country, as well as what might be done with the estimated 12 million illegal aliens already here. The majority of these illegal immigrants are deemed to be from Mexico, with the balance primarily from other poorer nations in Central America.

President Bush proposed a program of defining these people as "guest workers." His complicated proposal required these illegal American residents to step forward and identify themselves, be allowed to stay for up to six years if currently holding a job that no U.S. citizen wanted, pay a fine, be required to then return home, and then compete with other immigrants for any open U.S. jobs should they want to return to the United States. His plan allows these immigrants to apply for American citizenship via the traditional means.

It is no wonder the president's plan met with substantial resistance from both sides of the political aisle. The theory of the president's plan is one thing—human nature is something quite different. The vast majority of these illegal workers are not going to step out of the shadows and jump through a variety of hoops in order to clarify their status in this nation. In their minds, "if it ain't broke, don't fix it." Many members of Congress also see the eventual citizenship issue as unacceptable.

Other major proposals have called for much stronger enforcement of existing laws. These proposals include frequent raids on American employers likely to be employing illegal aliens, with the quick deportation of those workers who cannot provide solid proof of citizenship or viable documentation for being in the United States. Other proposals suggest that substantial fines or penalties for U.S. companies knowingly using illegal aliens should be mandatory. This logic suggests that many of these illegal workers will willingly return home if they realize that American employment opportunities are severely limited.

Where You Sit

Members of both major political parties have been inundated by their local constituents with opinions regarding the illegal worker issue. It is also human nature that one's view on the issue can be highly impacted by one's role in the economy.

Americans who have little or no employment contact with illegal immigrants are likely to support stronger enforcement of existing laws and rapid deportation of illegal aliens. They likely encourage or support politicians who promote such a proactive approach.

However, employers in such industries as hospitality, retail trade, construction, and landscaping strongly support the idea of leaving well enough alone. Many recognize that their ability to be adequately staffed requires the hiring of many immigrants.

Many of these employers would argue that their employees are not illegal immigrants, but in fact hold "documents" supporting their ability to work. Many of these employers might begrudgingly acknowledge that the usage of fake documentation is rampant. These employers might also suggest that it is not their responsibility to verify the authenticity of such documentation.

More Widespread Agreement

The one major immigration issue that draws more widespread support is that of enforcing American borders, primarily our southern border with Mexico. Most U.S. residents largely support curtailing the flow of additional illegal immigrants to the United States, even as they disagree regarding the issue of the estimated 12 million illegal aliens now here. Some of these citizens strongly support the building of a 700-mile double wall to limit access to the United States. Others would suggest that such a wall is too costly and would be largely ineffective.

Employment Impact

Major critics of the U.S. government's inability to limit the flow of illegal immigrants to this country argue that these people are depressing average American wages (by their willingness to work for lower wages) and also taking jobs that could be held by American workers. Such critics would suggest that American job and income gains have been severely impacted by the flow of illegal immigrants. The reality that the American economy is near full employment, with solid job gains and rising real wages in recent years, severely limits their emotional views.

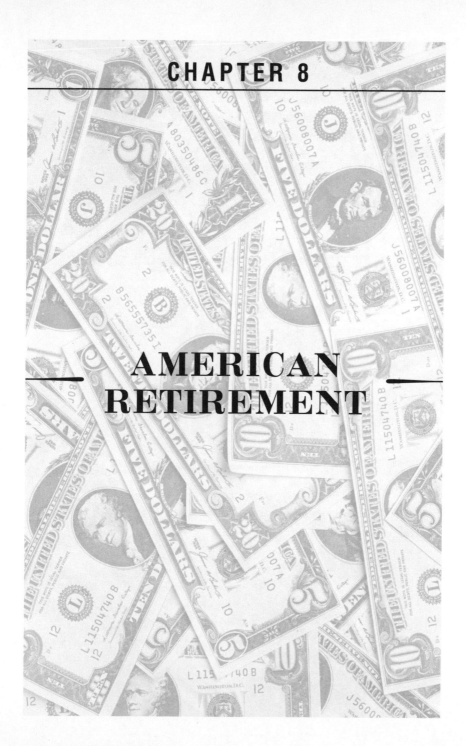

CHAPTER 8

AMERICAN RETIREMENT

BRIDGING

The nature of American retirement is likely to change dramatically. The prior notion of millions of American workers forced to retire at age 65, or setting their own goal of retirement at or prior to that age, is evolving. For many workers in coming decades, retirement at or before age 65 will be replaced with the process of "bridging."

Millions of Baby Boomers have seen a parent retire at age 65 or earlier with big plans for travel, leisure, and the like. Many retirees handled this change well. However, hundreds of thousands of retirees soon became bored with golf or travel or sleeping in. Many ultimately returned to the workplace, either to enhance income or just to keep busy and feel more productive. The sharp decline of the American stock market from 2000 to 2002 forced many of these prior retirees back to the workplace to rebuild or replace lost income or retirement funds.

Unfortunately for many, the skills they had utilized during their working careers in such employment sectors as advertising, education, financial services, government, health care, law, manufacturing, and sales were not in high demand in regards to older workers. Too many of these retirees soon found themselves as greeters at Wal-Mart or serving customers in the fast-food industry.

This is changing.

Two Major Changes

Two coincident developments in the economy will lead to a surge in part-time and flex-time employment for older workers. The first development is the substantial shortfall of skilled workers in the economy in coming years. An employer scramble already under way for both skilled and unskilled workers will enhance the relative value of older workers. Employers already struggle to attract and retain workers in such sectors as education, construction, health care, natural resources, and trucking. Such worker shortages will spread to more and more industries in coming years.

This monumental sea change is one that will greatly impact the American economy. The U.S. labor force is expected to grow at an average annual rate of less than 1 percent over the next 20 to 30 years, the slowest growth pace ever. Such minimal labor force growth in what is already a near-full-employment economy will create major challenges for employers of all shapes and sizes in coming years. Turnover costs, already painful, will rise even more as many companies see few applicants for open positions.

The second development is the desire of millions of Boomers to keep one foot in the workplace as we approach retirement age. Various estimates suggest that a majority of Boomers do not want to retire but also wish to "have a life" outside of the workplace. This development clearly complements the first.

Boomers *en masse* will express an interest in working part-time, such as three days per week, or working only mornings or afternoons, or perhaps two weeks on the job, followed by two weeks off. Others might work on a project for a month or two, with comparable time away from the job following a project's completion. Most of these "bridgers" will continue to work in their life skills area.

Enlightened Employers

Those companies that recognize this seismic shift in worker desires will be successful even as labor markets tighten further. Those employers who simply want to continue life as it was will face debilitating challenges in maintaining full employment, with many losing their most experienced older workers to more enlightened companies.

At the same time, the nature of work is changing. More and more work in service-providing industries is mental in nature, as opposed to physical in nature. In addition, people are living longer and living better. The process of older citizens bridging from full-time work to part-time employment in one's life skills area will be a major, major labor development over the next 20 to 30 years.

DEFINED BENEFIT PLANS AND THE PBGC

A rising number of American corporations have discontinued or frozen their "defined benefit programs" (including traditional pension plans) in recent years as a means of limiting retiree costs. Most of these corporations now provide a lump-sum payout to workers entering retirement or to those leaving the company. At the same time, the majority of these companies have introduced or enhanced the value of "defined contribution programs," primarily 401(k) plans, for their current and prospective employees.

Elements of the national media would have its readers and viewers believe that corporations are simply "trashing" retirement funding for their valued workers as a means of boosting corporate profitability. Many workers could see this result if they fail to take advantage of attractive features of alternative retirement plans.

However, those companies that highly value the efforts and skills of current and future employees will strongly encourage worker participation in defined contribution programs. More enlightened companies will also make retirement programs increasingly appealing so as to attract and to retain skilled workers in an enormously tight American labor market that is just around the corner. Those companies that resist such worker incentives will be destined for costly employee turnover expenses and even more costly employee attraction and training programs.

The PBGC

The Pension Benefit Guaranty Corporation (PBGC) is a federal agency created by Congress in 1975 to bail out domestic companies that default on pension obligations. The PBGC guarantees pension benefits for about 40 million American workers by assuming control of pension plans when and if companies in distress can no longer afford to fund such plans.

The government collects annual premiums of $31 for each worker covered by a company-sponsored "defined benefit" pension plan, or those that provide workers a set dollar amount each month upon retirement. Companies with plans deemed underfunded pay additional amounts. (The other major retirement programs are "defined contribution" plans, where an employer may match all or part of an amount withheld from their salary by a worker, such as in a 401(k) plan. It is important to understand the difference.)

The total number of defined benefit plans has fallen to less than 30,000 today versus 112,000 in 1985, according to the PBGC. These plans cover roughly 20 percent of private-sector workers today, versus 40 percent two decades ago.

Defined contribution plans cover more than 60 million U.S. workers today. These plans are not covered by the PBGC. These retirement plans, however, have the advantage that the assets are actually owned by employees. Such assets can be transferred from one employer to another during a worker's lifetime. Upon leaving a company, these retirement assets can also be transferred to a brokerage firm for safekeeping and investment advice.

The PBGC now collects more than $1 billion annually in premiums, an amount that is currently about $18 billion short of meeting its long-term commitments. The program actually saw its financial situation improve in 2006 tied to solid U.S. economic growth, strong corporate earnings, and the likelihood of fewer future "entrants" to the PBGC portfolio.

Many corporate pension plans were hit hard with declines in asset values (primarily stock prices) between 2000 and 2002. Traditionally, the PBGC was involved with companies that had failed, leaving current and impending retirees fearful of losing pensions. More recently, companies entering bankruptcy—but still operating—have been able to eliminate their pension costs before emerging from bankruptcy.

These companies are then free to operate and (hopefully) prosper. Taxpayers are then stuck with the tab for their workers' pensions. It is a cozy deal for simply too many companies.

Major Players

The steel sector was the first major American industry to play this game, with pension plans of more than 140 steel companies taken over by the PBGC. Today, the steel industry is doing better with much higher prices for steel during the past few years, tied in part to strong demand from China and India.

More recently, enormous losses within the airline industry led to similar moves by major carriers to lighten their pension loads. U.S. Air, United, Delta, and Northwest followed prior moves by Eastern, Pan Am, TWA, and other carriers. Their combined pension underfunding exceeds $13 billion in an industry that has collectively lost $40 billion since 2001. Better news finds that most major carriers returned to profitability in late 2006.

Who's Next?

Corporate debt previously issued by "Big 3" auto companies General Motors and Ford has been downgraded frequently in recent years by major credit rating agencies and now carries "junk" bond (or high-yield) status. These two companies are struggling to generate profits in a domestic and global auto market that is enormously competitive.

These companies have tens of billions of dollars tied up in annual health care and retirement benefits for their current workers, as well as for tens of thousands of retirees. Contemplation of eliminating their pension costs at some future point is also on their radar screens.

A worst-case scenario could eventually find General Motors and Ford proposing the same kind of pension shift to ensure their viability. The dollars involved at that point (current pension obligations exceeding $130 billion for GM and Ford alone) could blow the PBGC program out of the water.

What Can Be Done?

The most obvious solution would be to raise the annual premium per covered employee, which has already been raised to $31 in a series of steps. However, many members of Congress are only willing to support minimal future increases.

Changes enacted to allow struggling companies to fully fund their pension plans over a longer time horizon can also strengthen the PBGC. At the same time, any company that shifts its pension costs to the taxpayer, and then later returns to substantial profitability, should be required to contribute to the support of their pension obligations again.

Fair is fair.

401(k) AND DEFINED CONTRIBUTION PLANS

There are very few "no brainers" in the world of investing for retirement. One of the few is employee participation in 401(k) retirement plans (also known as *defined contribution plans*) offered by employers.

Another no brainer is financial participation in such a plan to the maximum percentage of salary matched by the employer.

The 401(k) plan has become the primary retirement vehicle for millions of American workers. It has the advantage that any contribution by the employee results in a lower level of current income tax liability.

Free Money!

A second major advantage is the "free money" provided by employers to those workers who participate. For example, assume a worker has a $60,000 annual salary. Also assume that the employer provides a 50 percent match up to 6 percent of the worker's salary. In this case, the employee optimally would choose to have no less than 6 percent ($3,600) of their salary withheld, resulting in $3,600 of lower taxable income, thereby providing significant tax savings. The company match of 50 percent of the first 6 percent of salary also results in another $1,800 contributed to the worker's 401(k) balance.

Too many workers might feel that such withholding is not an option because of financial commitments. In this case, the worker might have only 3 percent of salary withheld, resulting in only an $1,800 reduction in taxable income and only $900 in matching employer funds. In this case, the worker has not only minimized tax savings today, but also left a willing employer's $900 additional "gift" of free money on the table.

Ouch!

A third major advantage of 401(k) and other defined contribution plans is that of worker ownership. Such retirement funds, following short vesting periods, are assets owned by workers. They are "portable" to other employers if desired. Such funds cannot be taken or withheld by corporations facing financial distress, the types of companies that might terminate or freeze a traditional pension program.

A mistake made by many 401(k) participants is the temptation to cash out a 401(k) balance when shifting employers. The lure of new or unexpected spendable funds can be intoxicating. However, the penalty resulting in the loss of 10 percent of the 401(k) balance if cashing out (if less than 59½ years of age), the tax bite when converting tax deferred income to current taxable income, and the loss of growth in future retirement value for the funds can be painful.

Greater Knowledge

Critics of the shift to greater usage of 401(k) plans and other defined contribution retirement options decry the fact that the individual worker is required to make investment decisions, as opposed to corporate decision making regarding an investment mix with traditional pension plans. I would suggest that any program that provides greater incentives for workers to gain more investment knowledge is time well spent.

Such enhanced employee knowledge can also positively impact future financial decisions for millions of workers. In addition, recent legislative changes allow for greater access to advice and recommendations from investment professionals.

Recent Enhancements

The 401(k) has existed for 25 years, with individuals now holding more than $4 trillion in such retirement funds, a significant rise from prior totals. Recent enhancements to 401(k)s will only make the program more valuable in coming years.

The 401(k) program historically required a worker to voluntarily "opt in" to the program. This required some employees' understanding and initiative with paperwork and the psychological loss of income that otherwise could be received and spent. New legislation now allows companies to automatically sign new workers up for the program, a desirable change that will increase 401(k) participation and strengthen retirement savings for millions of workers. Such workers also have the ability to "opt out" at their discretion.

New rules also allow an automatic increase in the percentage of income going into such programs. For example, a plan might start out at 3 percent of beginning salary, with a rise to 4 percent after one year, to 5 percent after another year, and perhaps to 6 percent in the following year. Again, the worker has the option to alter or end their participation at any time.

New legislation passed in 2006 also allows for a wider array of investment alternatives for workers to choose from. Too many workers in prior years, with only limited knowledge of investment alternatives, selected a money market fund or employer stock as the default or primary investment.

New 401(k) rules allow "life cycle" mutual funds as the default investment. Such mutual funds provide for more aggressive investments into common stocks in a worker's earlier years, while also moving into more conservative investments such as U.S. Treasury notes as the worker moves closer to retirement.

Future Enhancements

Americans need to save more aggressively for retirement. Such a blanket statement is perhaps more true today than before, as traditional pensions are available for fewer workers.

However, just as the Congress passed legislation in 2006 to enhance the appeal of 401(k) programs to more Americans, so are additional savings incentives likely to be provided in coming years. Solid growth in 401(k) balances, more lucrative matching incentives by enlightened employers seeking to retain skilled employees in an extremely tight labor market, and new programs enacted by the Congress to boost retirement savings are in sight.

CHAPTER 9

GUARANTEED AMERICAN GROWTH INDUSTRIES

HEALTH CARE

U.S. economic strength or weakness leads most sectors of the economy to experience rising or falling employment levels over time. For example, the nation's manufacturing sector has seen total employment decline over the past two decades, even as total manufacturing output has risen. The culprit here has primarily been solid gains in worker productivity. The outsourcing of various jobs to lower-cost producers is also a factor. Employment totals in the construction and natural resources industries are typically tied in part to financing costs and prices of natural gas and oil.

Three major employment sectors will see their respective shares of total employment rise in coming years as compared to other sectors, even as the economy continues to experience ups and downs. These three industries will grow in economic clout compliments of the nation's 78 million Baby Boomers. The three sectors are health care, financial planning, and leisure and entertainment.

Common sense would suggest that the Boomer generation will play a major role in the expansion of health care services over the next 30 to 40 years. Such services will include the traditional combination of public- and private-sector health care providers, clinics, pharmacies, and hospitals.

In addition, you can add greater demand for plastic surgery of all types: Make these bigger or smaller. Build this up or trim this down. Tighten this up. Raise this. Lower this. The list goes on and on. Boomers will not go willingly into our senior years. We will fight it constantly.

Vanity of the Boomers? Off the charts!

Monthly health care premiums and consumer out-of-pocket costs have been rising faster than incomes for many years. Rising demand for health care services by Boomers, our parents, our children and grandchildren, and indigents will strain the current system as never before. It is not at all a stretch of the imagination to suggest that health care spending will carve out a larger share of GDP over the next few decades.

Such a move towards greater health care spending was already under way. However, the move will clearly be aggravated by an aging Boomer population. While this shift will be "good news" in regards to U.S. job creation, it will be "bad news" in terms of trimming overall productivity and optimizing utilization of resources.

For a majority of American families, a mortgage or rent payment has typically been the single largest monthly expenditure. For too many families, the monthly premium for health care insurance has moved into the top spot.

Our ability to slow the surge in health care costs is arguably tied to a handful of issues. The first would be the need to limit malpractice awards by the courts. Too many doctors have been forced to sharply boost their professional fees as a means of meeting sharply higher malpractice insurance costs. Too many doctors have simply decided to end their respective medical practices, while other formerly independent practitioners have moved back under hospital control in order to handle insurance premiums.

Medical tort reform is mandatory in order to get medical malpractice costs under control. High-profile medical problems attract aggressive attorneys who might gain an enormous financial award for a client (and for themselves), while resulting in higher malpractice premiums for all. Unfortunately, such a move under a Democrat-led Congress is unlikely as the legal profession is a major supporter of Democratic candidates.

Greater "control" of rising prescription drug costs is also necessary. Moves by various major retailers including Wal-Mart and Target to reduce costs of many generic drugs are a step in the right direction.

The Congress could have critical influence in this area by pressuring major pharmaceutical firms to limit prescription drug costs. Price controls, however, are not the answer.

Private-sector health insurance providers should have the ability to compete across state lines. Does it really make sense that a large health insurance provider in Connecticut cannot offer its services in Massachusetts or New York? Does it make sense that, for example, ABC Health Insurance of Oregon cannot compete with other providers in Washington or northern California, in theory providing more options and lower prices to consumers?

Imagine a world where interstate competition for financing of residential mortgages was not a reality. How much higher would mortgage interest rates be? How much higher would life insurance premiums be if buyers were limited to dealing only with insurance providers in their respective states?

A similar competitive reality is needed in the nation's health insurance sector. The cost savings to consumers could be impressive.

Rising utilization of health savings accounts is also in the nation's best interest. Greater familiarity with such programs and more aggressive promotion by employers would help limit health care costs in the American economy.

Wellness programs will also rise in prominence as employers "reward" employees who exercise and take solid steps to minimize health issues. Employers will also "penalize" employees who smoke or are overweight with higher health insurance premiums.

As health care costs continue their unrelenting march higher, we are moving unavoidably in the direction of a government-sponsored, nationalized health care system—I find the thought truly scary. Placing government in direct control of another one-sixth of the American economy does not lend itself to rising consumer comfort levels. One has only to look at a struggling Canadian universal health care system to draw such a conclusion (see Chapter 12).

FINANCIAL PLANNING

Baby Boomers *en masse* have not saved aggressively enough for our golden years. Such a painful reality is one that, in my mind, will drive millions of Boomers to save more diligently in coming years. In fact, recent data from various stock mutual fund providers has shown a solid rise in investment flows, most coming from Boomers. A similar mind-set is also likely to build as members of both Generation X and Generation Y increasingly recognize that *they* are largely responsible for the financial condition of their own retirements.

Millions of Boomers will also shift more aggressive investment money away from residential real estate back to the stock market. This is likely to continue as the news media and recent real estate market data suggest that most of the upward move in residential real estate values on both coasts and in the Southwest has largely run its course. This reality is one that drives my continuing view that the stock market will do very well in coming years.

Stronger Incentives

At the same time, the Congress is likely to adopt more savings-friendly legislation in coming years to provide greater incentives for both Boomers and younger generations to put more money away for their retirement. For example, recent legislation now allows companies to roll out Roth 401(k) plans to their employees.

The Roth 401(k) provides the means to put after-tax dollars into an account for the future. The advantage? After age 59½, withdrawal of both the principal and the interest is tax free. This program should appeal primarily to those who expect to be in a higher income tax bracket in retirement. Those expecting lower income tax rates in retirement might be better off with traditional 401(k) and IRA programs.

Members of all four major generational groups will further acknowledge that they may not have the necessary skills to develop a sound investment program for the future.

- How much should I save?
- What kind of investment return assumptions should I adopt?
- How much can I withdraw annually in retirement?
- What if I outlive my money?

These major anxieties will translate into greater use of investment experts, financial planners, and commercial bank trust departments. In addition, the ongoing shift within corporate America from offering workers defined benefit programs to defined contribution programs puts the onus on workers more than ever before to effectively manage their money.

Greatest Benefit

Members of Generations X and Y have the most to gain from the use of financial professionals. Too many workers of all ages have typically selected the most conservative or "safe"-sounding investment vehicle when selecting from various 401(k) options.

Placing retirement funds into lesser-risk money market funds or intermediate bond funds is logical for older workers, who favor greater preservation of principal and less investment risk as they approach retirement. However, younger workers with 30 or 40 or more years before retirement should have a majority of investment funds in stocks.

New defined contribution options wherein most 401(k) programs offer a "life cycle" fund is especially valuable to younger workers. Such funds opt for more aggressive investment options in a worker's younger years, while moving toward less investment risk as the worker ages. The employee simply needs to select a date in the future when retirement is likely and let the fund do the rest.

LEISURE AND ENTERTAINMENT

Travel, golf, college classes, new friends, cruising, hiking, new interests, spas, reading the classics, exercise, motor homes, the grandkids and great-grandkids, second (and third) homes.

You get the picture.

Baby Boomers will redefine the concept of retirement, just as we redefined or greatly impacted all other facets of life. Solid dedication to the first two growth industries discussed in the two prior sections will provide greater flexibility than ever before to enjoy life in our golden years.

Travel

Boomers will travel the world as no group before them. The sharp rise in ownership of vacation homes and motor homes will continue. More Boomers will take advantage of shared ownership of various leisure and travel assets, with a greater variety of time share and joint ownership options than ever before.

Tens of thousands of Boomers will establish second or perhaps primary residences in Mexico, Latin America, the Caribbean, and across Europe. Some will do so as a means of stretching retirement dollars, while others will do so as a means of experiencing other cultures firsthand. Other Boomers will routinely rent or lease a residence in Mexico or Europe or other destinations for one, two, or three months at a time. They will be able to enjoy other cultures, while avoiding potentially complex issues of residential ownership.

More options will also be available for Boomers and older retirees to live close to downtown areas in larger cities as a means of having close access to museums, shopping, the theater, and restaurants. Boomers will take advantage of such close proximity, while leaving the yard work or snow shoveling to someone else.

Universities, community colleges, and other sources will offer a wider array of classes and learning experiences than ever before, with many Boomers exploring interests and passions formerly displaced by the needs of generating incomes and raising families. Boomers will discover and develop talents never before considered.

Community Interest

More communities will entice retiring Boomers to live in their locales, recognizing the value they can bring to a community. The Boomer or Boomer parent in or approaching retirement age typically buys a local residence, shifts their financial resources to a local financial institution or brokerage firm, supports local retailers and restaurateurs, and creates little in the way of headaches for law enforcement personnel. One other major positive? They don't bring children that need to be educated.

Boomers will follow a path formerly explored by many of their parents. A rising share of senior housing and assisted living centers for older people will have a wider array of recreational and learning opportunities than ever before. Limited medical care will also routinely be on site or close by.

It's not your father's retirement!

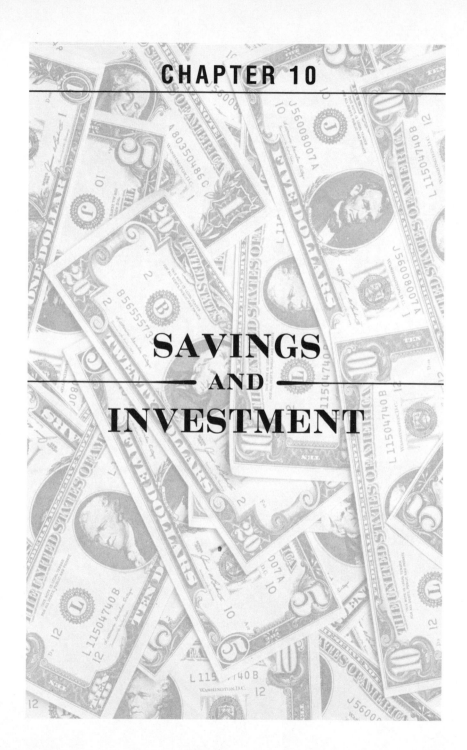

CHAPTER 10

SAVINGS

AND

INVESTMENT

THE STOCK MARKET

In the January 4, 2006, issue of our weekly newsletter, the *Tea Leaf* (see Figure 10.1), four reasons were given why the Dow average (at 10717 at year-end 2005) would not only break the all-time record of 11722 set in January 2000, but also trade above the 12000 level in 2006's second half. We noted the following:

1. The stock market would respond favorably to the Federal Reserve concluding its "water torture" approach to monetary policy. We suggested that the Federal Reserve would likely conclude its

FIGURE 10.1 *Tea Leaf*, January 4, 2006

Source: Thredgold Economic Associates.

aggressive monetary tightening on May 16, 2006, with "a 16th and likely final move" to 5.00 percent. We missed it by one. The Fed ultimately tightened 17 times between June 2004 and June 2006 and remained on hold well into 2007.

2. Numerous foreign stock markets had outperformed U.S. markets in 2005, which suggested greater relative value within U.S. markets.

3. A rising awareness among 78 million Baby Boomers that they had not saved aggressively enough for retirement would lead savings and investment higher, with billions of new dollars earmarked for stock market investment. This remains a long-term issue and is a key element supporting my view that the American stock market will do very well in coming years.

4. Billions of dollars would leave coastal and southwestern real estate markets and be invested in the stock market as further signs of a real estate bubble emerged. This should also drive stock prices higher in coming years.

Our Dow 10000 Call: A Chronology

The Dow Jones Industrial Average first closed above 10000 on March 29, 1999. Readers of the *Tea Leaf*, as well as its predecessor, *Dateline: The Economy* (while I was Senior Vice President and Chief Economist for many years of national banking giant KeyCorp), have known me as a stock market bull from day one. The following are direct quotes from various issues of the *Tea Leaf* of the past few years. At no point did we ever back away from our optimistic forecasts.

March 26, 1997—"This Fed tightening move could ultimately be one of the cornerstone events that lead to 'Dow 7500.'"

April 30, 1997—"People thought I was crazy during early 1994 when I was speaking around the country and predicting a 4000 Dow by year-end (missed it by seven weeks). Many thought the same a year ago (early 1996) when I predicted the Dow over 6000 by year-end 1996. I still expect 'Dow 7500' during 1997."

June 11, 1997—"As a long-time stock market 'bull' I have been very pleased to see the Dow trade above the 7500 level in recent days.... Where do we go from here? OK... here goes... at least 'Dow 7800' in the near term... and 'Dow 10000' before the turn of the century."

September 3, 1997—"I still expect Dow 10000 prior to the turn of the decade/century/millennium, although volatility will remain the norm."

October 15, 1997—"A Dow reaching 10000 by the turn of the century and modest annual growth in equity values thereafter seems reasonable."

March 11, 1998—"How high is high for the Dow? Maybe 9000 before the end of this year?"

September 23, 1998 (while the stock market was getting pummeled)—"I may be accused of drinking my own bath water, but I still expect new highs in the Dow average in 1999."

November 18, 1998—"... the (stock) market is still reasonably priced."

As noted, the Dow Jones Industrial Average first closed above 10000 on March 29, 1999.

Why Have We Been Bullish on Stocks for So Long?

Two Simple Reasons

The *first broad theme*—strong U.S. corporate balance sheets and rising U.S. corporate earnings. U.S. corporations dominate many major industries around the world. U.S. companies, large and small,

SILVER BULLET #4:
RISING STOCK VALUES

The stock market should continue to do well in coming years. More aggressive moves by Baby Boomers to build towards their retirements will provide billions of new funding monthly to the stock market.

At the same time, members of Generation X, as well as older members of Generation Y, will increasingly see the wisdom in saving more aggressively for their own later-life situations, understanding that *they* are responsible for their financial futures—not government and not employers.

have proven to be some of the most imaginative, flexible, powerful, and innovative on the global stage.

The rise in corporate earnings of the past decade has never been matched. In fact, powerful earnings growth of the past five years would strongly suggest that the stock market is substantially undervalued.

The *second broad theme*—the shift of the Baby Boomer from consumer to saver in a big way in coming years. The nation's 78 million Boomers are now in the process of moving from "the Age of Aquarius to the Age of Arthritis." Such a shift will continue to lead billions of new investment funds monthly into American equities.

Company stock buyback programs have also flourished in recent years. These announcements and follow-up purchases can be used by corporate executives to signal to market investors that they consider their share prices to be undervalued.

A differing view sees stock buyback programs as a temporary ploy to increase stock prices, but primarily an admission that a company does not have much in the way of growth potential. Otherwise, companies would spend their money on new plant and equipment and/or other corporate acquisitions.

Regardless of the view you might favor, the power of stock buy-back programs has been another element leading to rising stock prices. It is also a powerful means of limiting downside moves as company executives see opportunities to retire stock.

An interesting relationship is to compare the level of the stock market (as measured by the Dow Jones average) to U.S. GDP. The Dow first reached the 1000 level when American GDP was roughly $1 trillion. The Dow reached 10000 when U.S. GDP first approached $10 trillion, as shown in Figure 10.2.

Such a relationship today in an American economy with nearly $14 trillion of GDP suggests a 14000 Dow by 2008, with comparable increases in coming years. In fact, I would suggest the Dow will

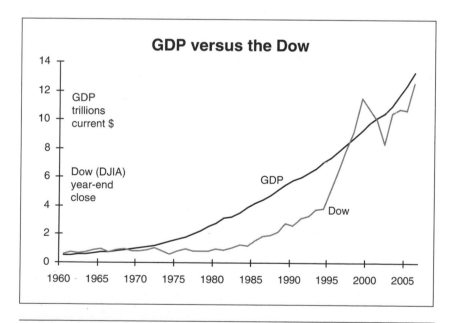

FIGURE 10.2   GDP versus the Dow

Source: U.S. Bureau of Economic Analysis and Dow Jones Co.

"outperform" GDP in coming years as millions of Americans save more aggressively for their golden years.

Can Dow 18000 be far away?

Four Corners

Anytime I address an audience and present an optimistic view of the stock market in coming years, an audience member will ask, "What about when the Boomers all start dumping stocks in a few years to finance their retirements?"

I respond to that question with an example. I ask the audience to view the room we are in as our entire economy, with four demographic groups represented in the room. One corner has the Greatest (or Silent) Generation. Some of these generational members at one table are slowly liquidating investments to finance retirements. Others are breaking even each year, while fortunate members continue to add to their portfolios.

Another corner of the room finds the Baby Boomers. The oldest Boomers can draw Social Security at age 62 in 2008. However, the vast majority of Boomers are in their 50s and late 40s. They will see more of their counterparts negatively impacted by changes in defined benefit plans. As a result, they will save more aggressively for retirement in coming years. Boomers will also inherit an enormous "pile of change" from their parents, with estimates between $12 and $20 trillion, the largest generational shift of wealth ever.

Another corner finds members of Generation X, simply put, the children of the Boomers. They have a mistrust of the future viability of Social Security. Most will also not collect from defined benefit programs, but will be more dependent upon their own and various employer contributions to defined contribution plans, including 401(k) programs. They have the advantage that the 401(k) program has been there for them since day one.

The same logic is likely to apply to members of Generation Y, simply put, the grandchildren of the Boomers. They will largely be responsible for their own retirements.

One other aspect is important. Assume for a minute that investment values in coming years do come under severe pressure as Boomers liquidate their investments in a big way.

What is happening around the world? Hundreds of millions of Chinese, Indians, Indonesians, and Malaysians are moving into their prime earnings years. They already save aggressively for the future. They will be more than willing to step into U.S. markets and buy U.S. assets at distressed prices.

The American stock market has been the premier place to invest for generations. It will retain that status in coming years.

SAVINGS

The national media has had a heyday in recent years, harping about the irresponsible behavior of Americans in regard to savings. As you have likely heard, "the savings rate" during 2006 was estimated at –1.0 percent, following the 0.5 percent savings rate decline in 2005, the first negative rates since the Great Depression, or more than 70 years ago. In addition, monthly measures of "savings" were negative in early 2007.

Not exactly.

As economists, we are dependent on various U.S. government agencies for most of the data we then try to interpret. Some of the data is quite good… some of the data is terrible. The "savings" data falls in the latter category.

Definition

"Personal savings," calculated by the U.S. Commerce Department's Bureau of Economic Analysis, is what is left after consumer incomes of all types are added up, then reduced by taxes. What's left, what you might refer to as take-home pay, is then reduced further by consumer expenditures of all types—a mortgage payment or rent, food, entertainment, and the like. The remainder is "savings."

One major problem with the savings data relates to gains on stocks. If you sell a stock at a gain, the capital gains taxes you pay are considered part of your "consumer expenditures." However, the monetary gain from the sale of the stock is *not* included in "consumer income." The Commerce Department indicates that it can't get that data fast enough, so the data is excluded. Whoops!

Another problem with the savings data? Any consumer funds applied towards a college education or valuable skills training in any employment area is simply considered consumer spending, while the funds used are certainly more worthy of classification as an investment.

Consumers today tend to think of their financial situation in terms of net worth (discussed later in this chapter). Powerful gains in most home values, combined with stronger performance of the stock market in recent years, have given consumers a peace of mind that building "wealth" for their future retirement or for the kids' college educations is working.

Low Rates

Consumers have also looked at the low returns on savings accounts and certificates of deposit during the past few years. The Federal Reserve pushed short-term interest rates to their lowest levels in 40 years between June 2003 and June 2004. Low short-term interest rates remained the norm even as the Federal Reserve tightened monetary policy during 2005 and 2006's first half. Resulting meager interest rates did not inspire savers.

Higher savings account and certificate of deposit interest rates available in 2006 and in early 2007 will help address the problem.

Many consumers have also recognized that a line of credit, such as a home equity loan, provides access for "emergency funding" needs, a role traditionally played by a savings account.

Concern

A review of savings data does cause some concern. Too many American consumers do not save enough for the future. Too many American workers do not take advantage of current retirement programs, especially 401(k) plans.

Too many young people want to match their parents' lifestyle of a nice home, nice cars, expensive "toys," and cool vacations. Too many people are too heavily buried in consumer debt.

Weakness in coastal and southwestern residential real estate markets, which developed in 2006 and 2007, should provide stronger incentives for millions of people to "save" more aggressively for retirement. Stock market strength of recent years, should it cease, could also induce more people to save by more traditional means.

Millions of people do not save aggressively enough for tomorrow. However, when considering the combination of savings *and* net wealth, millions of American consumers are in much better shape than the national media would lead one to believe.

NET WORTH

...is more than $55,000,000,000,000.

As American consumers, we are frequently scolded by the media regarding the massive amount of debt we have irresponsibly accumulated in recent years. We are told that we have a major need for instant gratification. We must have that new car, or that new outfit, or that new computer, or those new golf clubs or skis, or take that exotic vacation *now*—even if we have to borrow money to cover the cost.

Because of this constant media reinforcement, it is gratifying when information emerges that tells a different story, a story about millions of Americans who are conscientious spenders, millions of Americans who are saving for their children's educations, and millions of Americans who are saving aggressively for retirement.

The Federal Reserve releases a quarterly calculation entitled the Flow of Funds Accounts of the United States. This study estimates the value of all household assets, including homes, financial institution deposits, stocks, mutual funds, pensions, and equity in businesses. This combined value is then rubbed against all household liabilities, including home mortgage debt, home equity loans, other consumer debts, and unpaid life insurance premiums. The net difference represents the combined net worth of the American household.

U.S. household net worth at December 31, 2006, was $55.6 trillion, the highest total on record. It was also the 17th consecutive quarter where a new record was set. The $55.6 trillion net worth total was nearly one-third more than at the end of 2001 and more than three times the total in 1988.

The total had declined in 2001 and 2002 from the prior $43.6 trillion peak in 2000's first quarter. The meltdown of the stock market during those years (especially the Nasdaq) had hurt many investors, particularly those who were the most aggressive.

Homes and Stocks

The new record high has been driven by two primary factors. The first has been the sharp rise in home values across the country of the past few years. Home equity now represents roughly 41 percent of net worth, the highest percentage on record. The second has been the strong rebound of the American stock market of recent years.

Nearly 70 percent of American families now own their homes and have, in most cases, enjoyed sizable increases in their home values in recent years. The Office of Federal Housing Enterprise Oversight noted in late March 2007 that the average existing American home value rose roughly 55 percent over the prior five years. Even as home price appreciation slowed sharply, or even declined, in various coastal and southwestern markets in 2006 and early 2007, home values across many American communities continued to rise. Most forecasters expect overall prices to move essentially sideways in 2007, with a return to rising home values in 2008 and 2009.

An estimated 50 percent of American families now own stocks, a sharp rise from prior periods. Many now own stocks through their participation in employer-provided 401(k) programs. Solid gains in stock values of the past four years have sharply boosted the value of equity portfolios for millions of investors and retirees.

Median net worth (half of families with more, half with less) was slightly in excess of $100,000. The *average* family had a net worth near $500,000. This latter figure, however, overstates the typical family's net worth as significant wealth is concentrated among the richest households.

Theory, with considerable evidence, supports the idea that when our home and/or stock prices are rising, we feel wealthier. We are more willing to spend, a process known as the *wealth effect.* Movements of home prices have a greater influence on consumer spending decisions than do moves in stock prices. A solid rise in home values of recent years, combined with impressive stock gains, should continue to support reasonable U.S. consumer spending.

CHAPTER 11

MAJOR GLOBAL ISSUES

ENERGY

The United States imports roughly 60 percent of the oil used in this nation every day, a higher share than ever before. One positive aspect of this reality is that the primary sources of oil are more diverse than was the case during the heyday of Middle Eastern OPEC nations in the 1970s, which contributed then to the effectiveness of an oil embargo. Still, much of the globe's oil is under the control of nations that are not especially friendly to the United States, including Iran and Venezuela.

Oil prices during much of 2006 and early 2007 were above $60 per barrel, with a significant time where prices ranged between $70 and $78 per barrel. Various forecasts of oil eventually moving to $100 per barrel and above were prevalent. At that time, we were suggesting that oil prices would eventually settle around $50 to $60 per barrel.

Why? Because the Saudis, still the world's largest producer of oil, do not want prices sharply higher. Oil prices north of $70 per barrel raised the voices of those proposing greater use of natural gas, greater use of coal, greater use of nuclear energy, and greater moves toward energy conservation.

Prices north of $70 per barrel enhanced the call for more urgent moves toward hybrid and electric cars; more rapid use of new clean-burning diesel-powered cars; more rapid development of hydrogen cars; and greater utilization of wind, solar, and geothermal sources of energy. High oil prices boosted investment and government subsidies for ethanol development in the Midwest, with more urgent planning to utilize corn, grasses, weeds, and methane to generate energy.

High oil prices raised voices of those proposing greater investment into development of energy-rich oil shale deposits in the Rocky Mountain states of the West, with rising interest in investing into and agreeing to purchase greater amounts of oil drawn from energy-rich Canadian tar sands. High prices enlivened discussions regarding all means of reducing the usage of foreign oil and developing any and all promising forms of oil alternatives.

High prices enhanced arguments about the merits of developing oil and natural gas reserves in the Arctic National Wildlife Refuge (ANWR). High prices boosted interest in finding and developing promising sources of oil and natural gas off the continental shelf, as well as making high-cost exploration and production in the deep waters of the Gulf of Mexico more financially appealing. More optimistic voices talked of a national commitment to a Manhattan Project-style program to once and for all replace volatile foreign sources of energy, while making the United States much more energy self-sufficient.

The Saudis do not want us having those discussions. The Saudis are the primary swing player in regard to global oil output. In my opinion, they have and will continue to boost (or limit) oil production with the intent of maintaining prices in the $50 to $60 per barrel range. Such a level is one that both oil producers and oil users can live with, without providing the powerful incentives that much higher prices would in terms of developing oil alternatives.

A shortage of oil is not an issue. Recent estimates have sharply boosted proven and projected reserves of oil. Advancements in technology will allow a greater percentage of oil to be extracted from existing wells. Advancements in technology will enhance the means of reaching oil in formerly impossible locations, including miles below the ocean's surface. Advancements in technology will boost the energy efficiency of new automobiles, new homes, and new buildings constructed across the nation.

The future of energy will increasingly be found in those ideas we dream of today. OPEC's best days are in the past.

Different Views

The *consumer* in me would like to see energy and gasoline prices lower, with more traditional costs near $2 per gallon at the fuel pump. The *economist* in me would love to see oil prices rise to and stabilize around $100 per barrel for three to four years. Such high prices would not likely lead to recession, but would provide the most powerful and most urgent incentives ever for Americans to get a better handle on U.S. sources of energy.

Such high prices would strengthen the American mind-set that more oil and natural gas can be found in domestic locations and that greater successes in developing alternative sources of energy are available. High prices would provide the incentives to design and implement conservation steps that could be more effective in minimizing energy consumption in all types of appliances. Modest changes to construction procedures could help to minimize energy consumption in new homes, office buildings, and industrial sites.

Such high oil prices would aggravate the already high U.S. trade imbalance with the world. However, likely successes in trimming dependence on foreign sources of energy would, over time, lead the trade imbalance lower as our foreign energy bill declined.

Renewable sources of energy, including wind, solar, and geothermal, are unlikely to ever provide more than a minor share of overall energy. However, any positive changes are helpful. Each technological breakthrough in regard to more efficient and more cost-effective solar panels and more efficient wind turbines are all part of the solution. Technological enhancements to ethanol fuels (including changes to lessen the massive usage of water for each gallon of ethanol ultimately produced), coal liquefaction and coal gasification, hybrid automobiles, and hydrogen-based cars all contribute to a future less dependent on hostile foreign sources of energy.

What it takes is a nationwide commitment to such a goal. A consensus among and between government, private companies, and the American people is the first critical step in such a process. Higher energy prices would make that commitment easier.

CURRENCIES

Global swings in currency values are commonplace (although not as easy to predict or profit from as implied by all those newspaper, Internet, and television ads promoting get-rich-quick currency trading schemes). Day-to-day currency gyrations tend to be very small in nature.

Over time, however, relative changes in currency values can be large. Fluctuation in the value of the euro since being officially introduced in 1999 saw its initial value equal to near $1.18 in dollar terms. The euro soon fell to a value near $0.83 (a major European political embarrassment), only to appreciate later, only to fall again. The euro currency more recently appreciated again, trading near $1.25 to $1.35.

Different nations have different aspirations for their currencies. The Japanese tend to prefer currency stability or even a bit of yen weakness. They fear a stronger yen because it makes Japanese exports more expensive around the world, hurting domestic export industries.

A stronger Japanese yen does lead to lower import prices in Japan, helping to stretch consumer funds. However, lower prices are not necessarily viewed as a positive development in a country that experienced falling prices and a modest deflation during much of the past 10 years.

Euro weakness is viewed positively by European exporters, who can then sell their goods around the world at more attractive prices.

A weaker euro also appeals to the European travel industry, which delights at the prospect of more Americans and Asians taking advantage of attractive vacation prices.

European travel industry executives fear a strong euro as it boosts the costs of a European vacation for foreign visitors. Euro strength is also feared by goods producers as European exports become increasingly expensive around the world.

An additional impact of a weak euro? Imports coming into Europe are more expensive—potentially pushing inflation higher—which just might need to be met with additional short-term interest rate increases by the European Central Bank.

Currency Intervention

Why, for example, doesn't the Japanese government simply enter global currency markets to sell yen and buy dollars and/or the euro in order to help weaken the yen when market forces are pushing its value higher? They have done so periodically. In contrast, Europeans (and especially the United States) typically remain on the sidelines in the game of currency intervention.

The reality is that government and central bank interventions to strengthen or weaken currencies have been largely ineffective. A market move, for example, by the Japanese to sell $1 billion worth of yen to modestly weaken the currency has little impact in a global currency market where an estimated $3 trillion changes hands daily.

The U.S. Position

The "official" position of the U.S. government relative to its currency is typically a preference for a "strong" dollar. At various times, the global community's belief in such a U.S. commitment is challenged.

At times in the past, the United States favored a decline in the dollar's value as a means of addressing global trade imbalances, including during the mid-1980s. Such a time may again be at hand. One means of accomplishing such realignment is to have interest rate levels in Europe and Japan rising as U.S. rates are stable or expected to decline.

Over Time

The easiest path to reducing the enormous U.S. trade imbalance with the rest of the world is tied to a modestly weaker U.S. dollar and correspondingly stronger global currencies. Additional moderate dollar weakness versus other major currencies in 2007 and 2008 would make U.S. exports more price competitive around the world, leading American exports higher. At the same time, more costly imports into the United States from around the world, resulting from the reduced purchasing power of a weaker U.S. dollar, would provide an incentive for American consumers to buy fewer imported goods and a greater share of similar U.S.-made goods.

If such currency realignment is viewed by many as a positive step (given the enormous U.S. trade imbalance), why doesn't the U.S. administration voice its approval for such a move? Because such support for a weaker dollar could lead to a rapid fall in the currency, ultimately serving no nation's best interests. It seems best for U.S. politicians to talk a strong currency but be comfortable with moderate dollar weakness.

Holding Reserves

The U.S. dollar remains the global community's most desired currency, with the euro and the yen distant seconds. People around the world have traditionally saved "money" by holding U.S. dollars, either in the form of $100 bills or dollar-denominated financial instruments.

People make intelligent decisions as to their financial well-being in most cases, with more than half of all U.S. currency now held overseas.

The spread of U.S. dollars to more corners of the globe as "the currency of choice" is a validation of responsible U.S. monetary policy, political stability, and economic might in an enlightened global marketplace.

Values

Over time, I look at the relative value of a currency to a country as similar to the value of a stock to a company. An investor wants to hold stock in a company that has solid growth potential and higher earnings prospects. In a similar way, one can view the value of a currency.

An investor prefers to own the currency of a nation that has solid economic fundamentals, a competitive economy, and liquid investment markets. Such a view favors the United States and its currency.

A number of "old Europe" nations such as France are not so globally competitive, preferring to use rules and regulations to protect such internal industries as farming. Other European countries, including many of the former eastern bloc, have established policies to boost opportunities to be competitive with other nations and have welcomed their respective moves into the global mainstream.

Dollar Flight?

Various critics of the United States, both internal and external, decry the enormous trade imbalance the United States runs with the rest of the world. Such critics frequently talk of the impending dollar demise, where various central banks and investors around the world will soon dump the dollar and dollar-denominated assets.

I have less concern here. Any initial holders of dollars and dollar-denominated assets who wish to lighten up could easily sell select assets. However, in doing so they would depress the value of the dollar on global foreign exchange markets, as well as the value of select U.S. assets.

Any subsequent sellers would have to ask themselves whether they really wanted to suffer losses resulting from a weaker U.S. dollar and reduced U.S. asset values. Most would likely maintain their holdings. If, for example, a South Korean investor wished to sell U.S. assets and made a deal with a Saudi investor, the transaction would have no real impact on the United States.

In addition, where are investors who flee the dollar going to turn instead? Emerging markets, where bull markets can be powerful, but "Katy bar the door" in bear markets? A move into Japanese bonds yielding less than 2 percent? French growth stocks (yes, an oxymoron)?

Investors around the world will expand moves to diversify their global portfolios. Many major central banks have already begun this process. However, the U.S. dollar and U.S. dollar–denominated assets will continue to lead the way.

TRADE

The U.S. trade deficit in goods and services with the rest of the world has set new records in recent years, with recent imbalances exceeding $700 billion annually. U.S. companies export roughly $120 to $130 billion of goods and services to the world monthly. Other American companies and consumers import roughly $185 to $195 billion of goods and services from around the world. The U.S. appetite for autos, clothing, electronic goods, foods, and oil has led imports sharply higher in recent years.

It seems that each time the monthly trade deficit is reported, the national media implies that perhaps the American economy is just not very competitive. Why else would the United States import roughly

$2 billion more *each day* in goods and services from the rest of the world than we sell around the world? Consider this: As much as half of the U.S. trade imbalance is associated with U.S. subsidiaries in various parts of the world producing and shipping goods to the United States.

Many American politicians and economists wring their hands about the huge U.S. trade imbalance. I am not part of that group. In a perfect world, the United States would not run a large trade deficit or the even larger current account deficit. It is not a perfect world.

A Different View

Does the large U.S. trade imbalance suggest that American firms are just not very competitive with those around the world? To many "experts" it does. My view is quite different.

During the past decade, American consumers have largely benefited from solid U.S. economic growth, strong employment gains, higher stock prices, minimal inflation pressures, and sizable increases in home equity in most communities. American consumers who feel good about their employment and financial outlooks spend money aggressively on both domestic- and foreign-made goods and services.

Aggressive consumer spending in Japan—still the global community's second largest economy? Hardly. The "lost decade" of economic stagnation and plunging consumer confidence led Japanese consumers to save like there's no tomorrow, with millions of citizens limiting spending to basic needs.

Consumers across the Pacific Rim, including hundreds of millions in China, India, Indonesia, and Malaysia, see their countries experiencing major economic changes. As a result, these consumers spend cautiously and save aggressively, not knowing what tomorrow may bring. Similar issues are at play across the expanded European Union, Russia, former Soviet bloc nations, and nations across South America, all areas impacted by economic change.

The net result has been somewhat stagnant purchases of goods and services from the United States, an enormous amount of global savings, and the resultant huge U.S. trade imbalance. In my opinion, the large American trade deficit actually reflects U.S. economic strength and global economic anxiety.

For those who argue that this nation must run a trade surplus with the world, I say fine. All we need to get there is to have a long, deep, and painful recession, and we will. In fact, the last time this nation ran a trade surplus with the world, we were in recession.

This is hardly a good trade-off.

CHAPTER 12

MAJOR GLOBAL PLAYERS

THE PACIFIC RIM

China

Chinese economic growth of the past 30 years has been most impressive. China is a centrally planned Communist nation that has strongly embraced its unique version of free enterprise. By most measures, China now ranks as the world's fourth-largest economy, trailing only the United States, Japan, and Germany. Given its enormous population and vast natural resources, China could challenge Japan for economic leadership within the Pacific Rim by 2020.

Even as economic growth has been impressive, the Chinese face major challenges in coming years. One major issue is the growing income disparity between the newly wealthy and the majority of the population, especially those in rural areas. Tens of millions of Chinese citizens have seen strong economic growth boost their standards of living. However, similar numbers of Chinese have fallen further behind.

At the same time, powerful Chinese economic growth has led to serious issues with environmental damage. Too many cities are covered with clouds of polluted air, while too many rivers have been poisoned with industrial runoff. Greater environmental protection must be factored into the Chinese growth equation in coming years, a move likely to slow future economic gains.

China's financial system is also fragile, with Chinese banks holding vast amounts of uncollectible loans. Too many loans have been made based on political relationships and cronyism. At the same time, a vast lending network between Chinese citizens exists, which bypasses the banking system.

The Labor Issue

China's rise as a major manufacturing center has been impressive. However, the illusion of limitless and inexpensive labor availability in this nation of more than 1.3 billion people is simply that. Shortages of skilled labor, including managers of all types, are a reality today.

Engineers are in short supply. Such shortfalls of talent will become increasingly apparent as China continues its desired move from being a low-cost producer of apparel, games, toys, and various commodities to higher-skill, higher-cost output including electronics, steel, furniture, and autos. Land costs have also risen dramatically in recent years.

Substantial pressure remains in place from the United States and other major nations for the Chinese to allow their currency, the yuan, to sharply appreciate as a means of trimming its massive trade surplus with the United States. Critics maintain that the Chinese keep their currency at an artificially low value as a means of flooding the world with exports.

The Chinese have allowed this process of currency appreciation to occur at a modest pace. The Chinese have also made it clear that *they* will determine the pace of additional yuan appreciation in coming years, and will not have such decisions dictated to them by a U.S. administration or members of Congress.

The Dollar Issue

The flip side of China's massive trade surplus with the United States is their accumulation of hundreds of billions of dollars and dollar-denominated securities. Critics of such a development warn of the threat that the Chinese could, at some future point, decide to sell some or all such dollar holdings, triggering a massive fall in the dollar. In contrast, major dollar ownership is also the reason why the Chinese would *not* entertain such a move on an elaborate scale.

China's increasing role as a major global competitor will require certain changes to occur. The rule of law and copyright protection must be strengthened, while state-owned enterprises should eventually give way to greater private-sector participation.

I am asked frequently if the Chinese Communist leadership could stop the powerful entrepreneurial growth under way in recent years. My answer is to picture a powerful thoroughbred flying down the race track. Picture a tiny jockey holding onto the reins for dear life near the tail. The horse is the free enterprise explosion under way in China. As you might assume, the jockey is the Communist leadership.

Japan

The Japanese economy has been through the economic wringer over the past 18 years. Strong economic growth in the 1980s led prices of various Japanese assets including stocks, residential real estate, and commercial real estate to climb to unsustainable levels in the late 1980s, with most purchases utilizing borrowed money.

Powerful Japanese economic growth of the 1980s also led many experts to conclude that Japan's future domination of the global marketplace was a foregone conclusion. The 21st century was to be ruled by Japan. History didn't quite work out that way.

Picture the Dow at 2500

Picture the despondent and sickly nature of the U.S. economy if the Dow Jones Industrial Average were to fall steadily and painfully towards the mid-2000s over the next 14 years. Millions of American citizens would see their investment portfolios nearly wiped out.

Consumer and corporate spending would dry up on the way down as optimism of the past decade would be replaced with despondency and fear of what tomorrow may bring. Spending would nosedive, savings would rise, hundreds of thousands would lose their jobs, and pessimism would be rampant. This accurately describes the Japanese economy from 1989 to 2003.

The Nikkei Index, the primary index of Japanese stocks, topped out near 39500 in late 1989, during what turned out to be the peak of Japan's bubble economy. The index then headed south in an extremely painful and consistent way, bottoming out below 8000 in 2003's second quarter—a loss of nearly 80 percent and a loss of trillions of investor dollars.

Deflation

A laggard Japanese economy, a dismal stock market, and consumer pessimism eventually gave way to a period of deflation, or declining prices, beginning in 1997. This painful deflation, the first recorded by a major nation since the Great Depression, only added to the economic misery.

During a deflationary period, consumers and businesses have even less incentive to spend money. Spending is delayed in expectation of lower prices later. Business investment is curtailed because of expectations of declining sales. In addition, declining prices for goods and services, as well as residential and commercial real estate, are eventually followed by declining wages. Deflation continued for eight years, ending in 2006.

In the early 2000s, the Bank of Japan (that nation's central bank) belatedly responded with more aggressive moves to help stimulate the economy. Japan's political leadership also responded with increasingly aggressive spending plans to help revive the economy. Along the way, Japan's leadership incurred the largest national debt (as it relates to the size of the economy) ever recorded by an industrialized nation.

From Here?

Japan's economic recovery of the past few years has been led by more aggressive consumer spending, a rise in capital investment by

Japanese companies, and a surge in exports, primarily to China. Most forecasters expect reasonable growth to continue.

By most measures, Japan still ranks as the global community's second-largest economy. Japan still accounts for more than half of Pacific Rim economic output.

Modest Japanese economic growth expected in coming years is good news for its neighbors and for the United States. At the same time, much stronger economic growth in China suggests that the battle to be "top dog" in the Pacific Rim over the next 20 years will be worth watching.

India

India's emergence into the global mainstream has been somewhat overshadowed in recent years by the rise of China. Even so, the emergence of India as a world-class player in the 21st century is a major development.

The economically competitive nature of the Chinese and the Indians has changed the global landscape forever. The addition of roughly 1.5 billion potential workers from these two nations, combined with new labor competitors in other Asian lands and in eastern Europe, has seen a doubling of potential global workers.

India fell behind much of the world in the 1960s through the 1980s as it remained steeped in isolation. Relative standards of living in India versus other major Asian nations declined appreciably. This has now changed. Indian real economic growth of 6 percent to 9 percent annually over the past decade has been most impressive, but still in the shadow of the Chinese. Such growth is likely to continue.

Indian Strengths and Weaknesses

Competitive advantages versus China? One can start with an English-speaking population, a well-regulated stock market, a viable banking system, and ownership and copyright laws that are enforced. One can also focus on the fact that a majority of Indian growth is tied to meeting strong domestic demand, while China's economy remains focused on potentially volatile exports.

Impediments to growth? The list would include an outdated infrastructure, a poor-quality airport and highway system, and antiquated sanitation and water systems. The list would include a literacy rate that ranks among the lowest in the world, with a third of the population who cannot read or write.

At the same time, the contrasts are amazing. India has a higher number of information technology graduates than any other nation. As is well known, India is rapidly developing as a world-class center of R&D and various types of "white collar" and other professional jobs.

Outsourcing

India and American outsourcing go hand in hand. The American media provides one story after another of American companies that eliminate jobs in the United States in order to ship jobs halfway around the world. Such employment transplants have and will continue to occur. Many American companies, which formerly spoke quietly of such changes, now boast to Wall Street of immense cost savings.

However, such moves are becoming less valuable as wage levels climb sharply in India. Turnover rates are high. A shortage of skilled engineers in India has become a reality. Competition in terms of wage levels and skills from other nations is intense.

The connection between American technology centers and those in India is real, with hundreds of successful American companies having Indian nationals in leadership positions. It is not unusual for talented Indian entrepreneurs to keep one foot in the United States, with the other firmly planted at home.

India has seen its middle class of an estimated 300 million people expand rapidly. At the same time, hundreds of millions are destined for a lifetime of poverty. A caste system in existence for thousands of years remains firmly in place, especially in rural areas, limiting opportunities for tens of millions of residents. The AIDS crisis has impacted India in a tragic way.

India is a land of enormous opportunity. A more effective government focus on developing a world-class infrastructure could help lead India's emergence as a major economic power over coming generations.

EUROPE AND RUSSIA

Europe

Millions of European citizens find themselves in a fantasyland of "wanting to keep things the way they were" even as the fundamentals of the European style of government continue to crumble. Europe simply cannot have things the way they were.

Nevertheless, millions of residents of "Old Europe," in particular France, Germany, Italy, and Spain, refuse to accept the reality of enhanced global competition and unaffordable government-sponsored social programs. Their anxieties are many, including a substantial outsourcing of jobs, persistently high unemployment, a weak educational system, an aging society, a declining overall population, and new global competitors, especially China, India, and numerous eastern European countries.

Europeans face a barrage of issues, with limited means to escape economic sluggishness and high unemployment. Such was not always the case. European countries traditionally found many of their prized companies as formidable competitors. Many remain in this role, perhaps led by the German automakers. Reasonable levels of economic growth and low jobless rates were the norm in prior decades, but no longer.

The European Union

The broad objectives of blending together a unified Europe included the ability to compete globally as a more cohesive economic unit. Many successes were found, including the ability to dramatically reduce red tape and hassles involving trade among and between European nations.

The creation of a single currency for the European community has had mixed results. The euro currency enjoys broad acceptance as a major global currency (second only to the dollar). However, the loss of monetary flexibility among many of the smaller nations within Europe has been a major frustration.

Tomorrow in Europe

Growth prospects are modest as the European model of extensive social welfare, protected industries, high taxes, and few free market ideas remain its foundation. Companies by the thousands have shed jobs in Old Europe even as they added jobs in the Czech Republic, Slovakia, Romania, and Hungary.

Fewer Bodies

Europe also faces an actual decline in population. The European birth rate (as in Japan and Russia) is well below the "replacement rate" of 2.1 children for each woman of childbearing age. For western Europe as a whole, the birth rate is now 1.5, with lower rates in Old Europe. A continuation of such low birth rates for years to come would lead overall populations sharply lower, and threaten the ability of taxpayers to finance future government social spending.

In all likelihood, stronger overall population growth is expected. However, it will be the result of higher birth rates in poorer Eurozone countries and stronger migration (both legal and illegal) into France, Germany, Italy, Spain, and so on.

High levels of Eurozone unemployment compensation and welfare have traditionally provided many citizens with an ability to survive while lacking jobs. Many have lived at public expense for years. Average jobless rates of 9 percent to 10 percent in Germany and 8 percent to 9 percent in France compare to rates half as high in the United States and Japan.

Life in Old Europe includes the "haves" (older high-wage unionized workers) and the "have nots" (millions of younger people who will move between limited employment opportunities and more "comfortable" jobless benefits than found in most parts of the world)—not a pretty picture for the young.

Eurozone Expansion

Bigger is better—or so has been the mind-set of European leaders. The European Union comprised 12 member nations a decade ago. Membership today is roughly 25 nations, representing more than 450 million people. A cohesive group? Tens of millions of new member citizens speak different languages and represent vastly different cultures, including rising Islamic populations.

Citizens of richer nations seethe at the addition of 10 mostly poor nations during the past few years, with rising anxiety about the loss of their higher-wage jobs to those poorer countries that feature much lower wage levels.

Facing Reality

There is a quiet realization building across European political and business circles that in order to be competitive with North American and Pacific Rim companies, European companies must have greater flexibility in terms of hiring/firing practices, more open competition, and wider use of production incentives for workers. Lower tax rates and less government are also viewed as necessary.

Some progress is being made, with more upbeat growth prospects for those nations willing to embrace change. Data also suggests that a greater share of Eurozone growth is coming from rising domestic demand, a favorable development should the euro continue to appreciate versus the dollar in coming years.

The enormous unemployment rate disparity between Europe and the United States/Japan comes down to the issue of the entry and exit of labor in a free market. Pro-union governments and powerful labor unions have distorted the European labor issue. The reality is that once a company hires an additional employee in various countries, it is almost impossible or very costly to ever let them go.

So what do rational European company managers do in this hostile labor environment? They utilize alternatives to new hiring, including more overtime for current workers, greater use of automation, more use of less costly Central European or Pacific Rim labor, and greater investment into non-European companies that operate in more business-friendly locations.

Liberal European governments blame their high unemployment rates on job-reducing technology and increased competition from countries where wages are lower. However, they are unable to explain why unemployment rates in the United States and Great Britain are so much lower—countries subject to the same competitive pressures.

The realities of high unemployment and limited economic growth prospects are finally leading labor leaders to the bargaining table, with particular progress in Germany. German workers in various industries, principally manufacturing, have agreed to greater flexibility in exchange for promises that jobs will be maintained.

German workers are embracing more flexible and longer work weeks. In addition, more and more German and other workers are trading fixed (but declining) bonuses for something commonplace in the Western world—profit sharing. The ability of European nations to enjoy solid growth expectations in coming years is tied in part to such labor flexibility.

Russia

A quick question: Which nation's economy would be the least similar to that of Russia?

Saudi Arabia… Canada… the United States?

The correct answer would be the United States. Given the realities of today's global energy markets, you can think of Russia as perhaps most closely identifying with the Saudi Arabian economy as far as the critical nature of oil revenue and oil reserves.

You can also think of Russia as identifying closely with Canada as far as the vastness and reach of its geographic landscape. Even after the breakup of the former Soviet Union, the country of Russia today still expands over 11 time zones and is the largest in land mass on the planet.

While vast in geographic scale, the nation is much less an economic power. Even with the surge in oil production and oil revenue, Russia fails by most estimates to make the "top 10" nations as measured by annual economic output.

The Russian economy has made major economic strides in recent years, even as its versions of democracy and freedom have sharply retreated. Volatility of the past 15 years has not been for the faint of heart. Political corruption, economic chaos, bribery, violence, and money laundering are all taken for granted in the former Soviet Union.

Doing business in Russia is a major challenge, with the rule of law limited in many cases. The Kremlin has been more than willing to bend rules in order to restrain the influence of many internal rivals.

Today's Russia is a vibrant economy, which enjoys the intoxicating effect of enormous oil and natural gas revenue. Russian oil exports now trail only those of Saudi Arabia. Russia is deemed to have substantial untapped reserves of oil and natural gas. The nation could be a critical swing player in oil production in coming years, while Russia's natural gas reserves are the largest on the planet.

Much of Europe is dependent on Russian natural gas to heat their homes. These nations are vulnerable to supply shutdowns if they defy Russian desires. The Russians may find that natural gas is a more powerful weapon than bombs ever were to achieve their political goals.

Fewer Comrades

All is not well, however, in Russia. The nation suffers from one of the global community's lowest birth rates, an issue that Russian political leadership is trying to address with financial incentives for women to have more than one child. The Russian population declined from roughly 149 million people in 1992 to 142 million in 2006.

The Russian population is currently declining by approximately 700,000 people annually. Over a period of years, such a decline would have a very detrimental impact on generating tax revenue for various government programs, as well as crippling the workforce.

Russia has not been immune to population declines before. Deaths of millions of Russian citizens occurred in World War I and World War II. Other periods of violent political purges and famine led to the deaths of millions of Russians.

Population Dispersion

Another quick question. Name any major Russian city besides Moscow and St. Petersburg (formerly Leningrad). Only two Russian cities have more than two million people, while the United States has 14 such cities. The other top five Russian cities of Novosibirsk, Nizhny Novgorod, and Yekaterinburg don't exactly roll off the tongue. The point? The Russian economy is significantly rural and smaller city in nature, versus the larger city life so prominent around the world.

The Russian people favor order above all else. The Russian people have seen their standards of living climb sharply under more recent political leadership, with a sharp rise in average per capita income in recent years.

Coming and Going

Russian citizens with money to spend are a major plus for European vacation destinations. Tens of thousands of Russian citizens now travel frequently, with major efforts developing by various European destinations to attract this new source of spending.

In contrast, visitors to Russia are in decline. The high level of crime and violence limits travel interest by millions of Europeans. Various Russian communities are attempting to boost foreign visitation by targeting the criminal element that focuses on tourists.

NORTH AMERICA

Canada

Canada has come a long way in terms of economic performance in recent years. It is the only member of the Group of Seven nations (Canada, France, Germany, Italy, Japan, the United Kingdom, and the United States) to be running a budget surplus. It is also, by definition, the only Group of Seven member to actually be paying down some significant portion of its national debt.

In Balance

Canadian political leadership learned some valuable lessons in recent decades, with positive results now evident. When faced with budget deficits in, for example, the 1980s through the mid-1990s, the classic Canadian response was to raise taxes to cover the shortfall.

You can raise taxes "from hell to breakfast" with little likelihood of balancing a budget. The Canadians finally realized that the cure for budget deficits was to constrain the growth in spending. Balanced budgets are expected in coming years as well.

Canadian economic growth in recent years has been nearly on par with that of the United States. At the same time, the Canadian unemployment rate declined to the "low-to-mid-6" percent range—high by American standards, but the lowest Canadian unemployment rates in 30 years.

Rising Home Values

Strong U.S. economic performance of recent years, combined with extremely low mortgage financing rates, led to some of the strongest U.S. home price appreciation on record before more recent cooling. A similar result occurred north of the border.

Solid Canadian economic growth has led to a sharp rise in Canadian housing prices. Home values have risen most noticeably in western Canada, where growth has been particularly impressive as a result of high energy and commodity prices.

Headwinds

Solid Canadian growth is likely to continue, led by strength in consumer spending. However, the economy faces three powerful headwinds. The first has been monetary tightening moves by the Bank of Canada, the Canadian central bank and equivalent of the Federal Reserve in the United States. The Bank of Canada felt compelled to push its key short-term interest rate higher in a series of moves beginning in September 2005. Inflation containment is a major issue on both sides of the border.

The second headwind is high energy costs. While high energy prices have led to a surge in investment and employment in the natural resource sector so critical in western provinces, such higher prices are also paid by Canadian consumers, trimming spending in other areas.

The third headwind is a strong Canadian dollar, which rose sharply versus the U.S. dollar in recent years. The Canadian dollar, or "loonie," appreciated more than 25 percent versus the U.S. dollar from 2004 through early 2007 and was at a 28-year high versus its American counterpart.

The result has been significant pain in the Canadian manufacturing sector. Canadian manufactured goods become more expensive in the U.S. and around the world when priced in many other currencies. Job losses in manufacturing have been sizable. Powerful productivity gains in the sector should help minimize additional job losses in the future.

The strong loonie has also led to a sharp decline in the number of Americans vacationing and shopping in Canada in recent years. Many Canadian resort communities and retailers dependent upon U.S. visitors have suffered. At the same time, the crossover of Canadian visitors and shoppers to northern U.S. communities has been robust. Canadian dollar strength has made American products and services bargain priced. Another incentive has been overall sales tax levies and gasoline prices, which are lower in the United States.

Trade-offs

As with most factors within economic study, there are winners and losers on both sides of most any issue. High energy prices, and the expectation of many that reasonably high prices are likely to continue, have led to an enormous surge in investment into developing the oil-rich tar sands so prevalent in western Canada.

Good news finds Canada now sitting on what are generally agreed to be the second-largest oil reserves on the planet, exceeded only by those of Saudi Arabia. Good news includes the creation of thousands of high-paying jobs, with a severe shortage of skilled workers already a reality. Good news also finds that oil production from the sponge-like sands, already exceeding one million barrels daily, could rise sharply in coming years if global oil prices remain high. Such growth in output now finds Canada as the largest supplier of oil to the United States.

Bad news finds a high environmental toll as a result, with enormous demand within the sector for water and natural gas. I am one who is a strong believer in the power of technology to address problems. New technology to lessen the impact of energy production on the environment is both expected and welcome.

Universal Health Care Pain

All is not well in Canada, however. The government-funded health care system is extremely expensive, largely broken, and in need of resuscitation. The four-decade-old system is a major frustration to Canadian citizens. Ordinary citizens are subjected to lengthy waiting lists for doctor visits, especially to see any type of specialist.

Wealthier citizens routinely cross the border into the United States to get more immediate, and in many cases, higher-quality health care. Canadian doctors and nurses continue to flee the system in droves to practice in the United States or elsewhere in the world.

Mexico

Twelve million illegal residents, representing perhaps 10 percent of the Mexican population, now find themselves in the United States, most working and living in the shadows of the underground economy. The issue of illegal immigration will be a major American economic and political issue as the 2008 election cycle approaches.

The Mexican economy has grown at a 3 percent to 4 percent real annual rate since 2004, in line with U.S. growth, following a period of weakness during the prior few years. However, the demands of rapid labor force growth and a high level of unemployed people requires a stronger growth pace.

Mexican economic growth needs to run at perhaps a 6 percent to 8 percent real annual rate in order to provide valuable work opportunities for the 1 million new labor force entrants annually. Greater employment opportunities in Mexico at fair wages are the easiest means of limiting the flow of illegal immigrants to the United States. After all, the U.S.-Canadian border is not teeming with unsatisfied Canadians seeking "a better life" in this country.

Flow of Funds

A major component of Mexican gross domestic product is the flow of funds from the United States. This flow of funds, estimated to exceed $20 billion annually, provides tens of thousands of Mexican families a valuable source of income. This income is largely free of government control. The funds provide financial support and the means to enhance living standards. In some cases, the funds also provide Mexican families the means to start or expand a small business.

A Plunging Birthrate

One major development likely to lessen the flow of illegal immigrants to the United States from Mexico in coming years is the plunge in the average birthrate of Mexican women. Forty years ago, the average Mexican woman had seven children, among the highest birthrates in the world. That number is now approaching two children, directly in line with the birthrate of women in the United States.

Such shrinkage of the average Mexican family size will provide the opportunity for more affordable educational access for many young people than before. Such access can provide the base for a rising standard of living in Mexico for millions of tomorrow's citizens.

Do as I Say

Mexican political leaders seek expanded access for their citizens to locate better jobs in the United States than those available at home. These same leaders sing a much different tune when considering the treatment of illegal immigrants entering Mexico from even poorer nations, including Ecuador and Guatemala.

Many Hispanics and Latinos illegally entering Mexico from poorer southern nations, perhaps seeking eventually to find employment in the United States, are many times met with harsh treatment by Mexican police or military personnel. Many are forcibly returned to the border, while others face prison terms.

Fierce Competition

Mexican politicians and business leaders saw a great opportunity in passage of the North American Free Trade Agreement (NAFTA) more than a decade ago. Initial success did take place, with substantial employment growth in *maquiladoras*—export assembly plants—across the Texas border.

China then raised its aggressive stature, with manufacturing costs sharply below those in Mexico. Thousands of jobs were lost, primarily in manufacturing. Modest success now finds a number of these facilities reopening, focused on higher-quality goods earmarked for rapid shipment across the border into the United States.

Mexican business leaders are also focusing efforts to attract American "outsourcing" jobs to the country. Supporters note the wide array of people who speak English comfortably, the rising economic clout of the Spanish-speaking Hispanic population within the United States, and the fact that Mexican time zones are identical with those in the United States.

Down the Road

Mexico must implement major reforms to various government policies in order to boost economic growth to more desirable levels. Inflexible labor laws must be modernized, while a weak tax collection system must be strengthened. Widespread government corruption must be addressed.

The Mexican oil sector, totally under governmental control, must be loosened to attract the outside investment needed to provide critical maintenance and opportunities to find valuable new oil deposits. New leadership must streamline government, with moves toward greater efficiency of state-owned enterprises.

Mexico has made progress. Construction has risen, while consumer spending is on the rise. The national debt has declined. The currency is more stable than before, while inflation pressures are moderating.

Despite these successes, major challenges remain. Unemployment continues at stubborn double-digit levels. Too many Mexican citizens see only limited opportunities within the country, with too many seeking greater opportunities north of the border.

Perhaps the word that has most characterized the Mexican economy in recent decades has been *potential*. The Mexican economy has occasionally exhibited flashes of brilliance, only to then self-destruct—one more time.

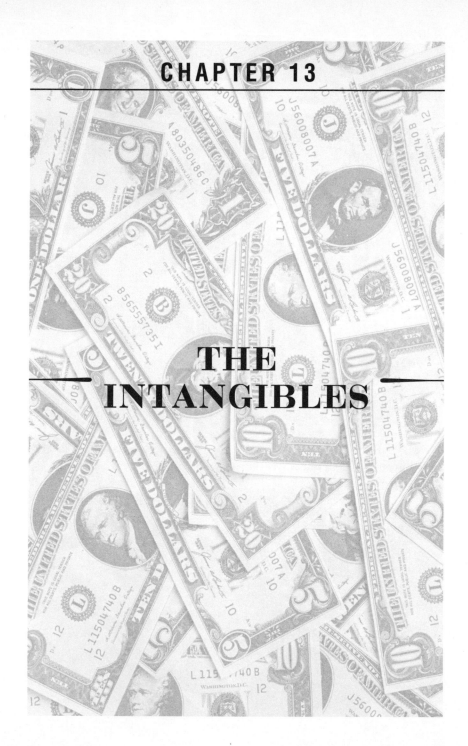

CHAPTER 13

THE INTANGIBLES

COMPETITION

One important factor supporting my view of an American economy that can and will perform well in coming years is that of competition. The highly competitive American economy has faced a series of major competitors in its relatively brief history. This is especially true in the post–World War II period.

One of the first was Japan. The rise of Japan from a war-ravaged nation in the mid- to late 1940s to a world-class economic player over the past 25 years has been remarkable. This nation focused on manufacturing and exports as a means to enhance economic growth and boost living standards.

Remember in the early 1990s when "the common wisdom" in the United States suggested that our school-age children needed to learn to speak Japanese? Why? Because Japan was going to rule the economic world. While stumbling badly in the 1990s, Japan remains the global community's second-largest player.

Russia staged its own major recovery from the devastation left by World War II. This nation followed a different path to global importance, one based on central control, military intimidation, and limits to individual freedoms. This superpower during much of the 20th century's second half ultimately succumbed to a military spending contest with the United States, which had the economic diversification and depth to afford such an arms race. The Soviet Union did not, and this led to its collapse in 1991. More recently, a revived Russian economy has resurfaced, this time "fueled" by vast amounts of oil and natural gas.

The blending of a dozen European nations into a more cohesive economic and political unit was supposed to curtail U.S. economic dominance. Instead, frequent squabbles between nations, large budget deficits, disagreements as to future membership, and the fact that such nations as France were not all that competitive (without government protection of various sectors) rendered European economic status to the second tier. Greater reform is necessary for Europe to become truly competitive, a process finally taking place.

The rise of China and India were the primary global themes of the past decade. China's move towards greater economic freedom and incentives, still under a Communistic umbrella, has been most impressive. In the eyes of many, it is China that is destined to rule the 21st century.

Not so fast.

Chinese economic potential as measured by population and natural resources is indeed formidable. Powerful industrial output has led tens of millions of Chinese to boost their standards of living. Still, the Chinese economy faces major hurdles in coming years.

Hundreds of millions of Chinese farmers and peasants continue to struggle with poor living standards, especially in more rural communities. The Chinese banking system faces massive losses. The Chinese people are slowly recognizing that strong economic growth is not so attractive if the trade-off is poisoned rivers and dangerous air pollution in major cities.

China will likely be the greatest economic rival faced by America in coming decades, especially in the goods production area. However, dealing effectively with its own serious challenges will require a slowing of its economic growth pace in coming years.

India will remain a formidable economic power, especially in the white collar and high-skills sectors. The nation's industrial base will also rise. However, its challenge of dealing with hundreds of millions of poor and largely illiterate people will limit economic dominance. The bloated and ineffective government bureaucracy will impede critical reforms.

Brazil, Indonesia, Malaysia, and Mexico are expected to rise in global economic position. Still, each has its own laundry list of challenges that must be faced along the way.

A key to global economic growth potential will be the need for political leaders around the globe to avoid the temptations of trade restrictions with other nations. All nations can see living standards rise as long as the global economic pie continues to grow.

God forbid you fill a room with economists. The only factor that we will largely agree on is that any steps taken to build bridges to global trade are positive—and any steps taken to establish barriers against global trade are negative.

We will disagree on everything else.

EMOTIONS AND CONFIDENCE

Economics is simply "the study of life" and the choices we make. Human emotion is perhaps the strongest force in the economic and financial environment. It gets its appropriate level of respect in the real world—and a very short shrift in the land of academia. Human emotion—in this case, the need to keep up with the Joneses, the drive to get a great deal, and the drive to make a killing on an investment or a property—can contribute to positive or negative developments in the economy.

Fear and Greed: Stocks

Emotion at times can be the primary driver of stock prices, whether up or down. The powerful emotion of fear can motivate holders of stocks or other financial assets to sell, at times regardless of the price received. The equally powerful emotion of greed can motivate investors to buy various assets, even when the inner voice might suggest the price is too high. Only later, in many cases, can investors recognize that they were "caught in the moment" and let emotion drive their actions.

Greed was clearly center stage during the second half of the 1990s and the first quarter of 2000, especially in regard to Internet stocks and the Nasdaq. Investor greed drove many Internet-based companies to sky-high stock market valuations, even as many of these companies lacked profitability or a reasonable chance to become profitable anytime soon. The overall Nasdaq was pushed to a high of 5049, much higher than many investors and market players deemed logical or possible.

At such unsustainable levels, fear soon became the more dominant emotion. The fear of millions of investors eventually pushed the Nasdaq down to 1113, a decline of nearly 80 percent. Hundreds of thousands of investors saw major losses in their retirement portfolios, requiring them to either stay in the workforce longer or return to gainful employment in order to rebuild damaged portfolios.

Fear and Greed: Real Estate

A similar greed-based rise was also found in the nation's real estate market in recent years. Tens of thousands of investors pulled their funds from the stock market and sought a new avenue to riches— real estate was just the ticket.

The decline of both short-term and long-term interest rates from 2001 through 2003 provided thousands of home buyers with the opportunity to purchase their first homes. Tens of thousands of existing homeowners took advantage of the lowest home financing rates in 40 years to trade up to more valuable properties.

The Flippers

In addition, investors and speculators by the thousands began to push real estate values higher. Many of these investors, commonly known as *flippers*, took advantage of extremely low short-term financing rates to buy additional properties.

It was not uncommon in hot real estate markets on the East Coast, the West Coast, and in the nation's Southwest for flippers to appear at announcements of new single-family and condominium developments, with the intent of buying multiple properties. Many of these flippers were successful in immediately bumping prices higher, and were able to pocket significant profits with limited risk.

Many of these flippers were also quietly aware that if they took excessive risk and were ultimately forced to liquidate their positions, the opportunity to file for bankruptcy protection was available. This option, however, was tightened up considerably by the Congress, effective in October 2005.

Other flippers came belatedly to the game in late 2005 and 2006 and were ultimately stuck with multiple properties to finance, with limited potential buyers. Many of these flippers, as well as thousands of more legitimate homeowners, faced the bleak task of trying to unload properties at a time when many others investors were engaged in the same process. Their financing plight was made worse by the impact of 17 monetary tightening moves by the Federal Reserve through June 2006, pushing the Fed's key federal funds rate from a 46-year low of 1.00 percent between June 2003 and June 2004 to a 5-year high of 5.25 percent.

Confidence

One of the most powerful forces in the economy is consumer and corporate confidence, or the lack thereof. Consumers who are confident in their ability to maintain a job, to maintain various payments, and to maintain or enhance their economic and financial position are those willing to spend money.

The same is true for corporations, both large and small. If company executives or a small business owner are not confident in their ability to manage growth, to generate profitability, and to grow, their decisions will reflect caution. They may pass on new opportunities for growth or new markets and simply hunker down to await whatever challenges surface.

Confidence can be greatly impacted by change or the threat of change. Hundreds of millions of consumers around the world, including those in India, China, Malaysia, Indonesia, and eastern Europe, have seen major changes in their recent lifetimes. Many have seen their standards of living rise, while many have experienced the opposite.

Change fills many people with anxiety, perhaps the opposite of confidence. As a result, hundreds of millions of consumers around the world spend cautiously and save as much as they can, not knowing what tomorrow may bring. Higher confidence levels would support stronger global consumer spending, helping to reduce the U.S. trade imbalance with the world.

The American Consumer

The primary contributor to strong U.S. economic growth of recent years has been the U.S. consumer. While the media typically focuses on the Googles, Fords, and General Electrics of the world, the American economy is a consumer economy, with consumer spending accounting for two-thirds of all U.S. economic performance.

A confident U.S. consumer—supported by strong job creation, minimal inflation, and rising incomes—spends money more aggressively, contributing to solid gains in corporate sales and profitability. Conversely, an American consumer concerned about global financial volatility, gyrating U.S. stock prices, political scandal, and rising corporate job cuts spends money more cautiously, contributing to slack growth, or actual declines, in corporate performance.

THE POWER OF INCENTIVES

Let's face it... economics is boring, confusing, frustrating, and intimidating in the hands of an amateur. It is even worse in the hands of a professional. I came across a four-word definition for economics that is perfect—people respond to incentives.

Free enterprise and capitalism are not perfect—but they are the best systems in the world. You have an incentive in a free enterprise economy to work hard, to work smart, to work late if necessary, to save and invest wisely, to help your kids get a good education.

Everything we do in a free-enterprise economy is incentive and reward based—that is why it works.

Communism—socialism—these offer very few incentives. Think about it. Fifty years ago, half the world was under communistic control in it purest form. Now that number is mere handfuls.

Winston Churchill said it best, "The inherent vice of capitalism is the unequal sharing of blessings. The inherent virtue of socialism is the equal sharing of miseries."

People respond to incentives.

CHAPTER 14

THE FUTURE

THE AMERICAN CENTURY...
AGAIN

My optimistic view of the American economy is based on four critical assumptions expressed in previous chapters and reprised here.

Silver Bullet #1

American Workers Will Prosper in Coming Years as a Result of Extremely Tight Labor Markets

On balance, extremely tight U.S. labor markets expected during the next 20 years will sharply increase the real (inflation adjusted) earnings of tens of millions of American workers, while also enhancing the value of their benefit and retirement programs. Successful companies in all industries and of all sizes will strive to minimize costly employee turnover and reward key employees. This is a critical and major departure from labor conditions that existed during most of the past 20 years.

Silver Bullet #2

Bipartisan Political Cooperation Will Soon Address the Future Entitlement Funding and Benefit Imbalance

This nation will reach a point in coming years when politicians are simply forced by the pressure of powerful financial markets and by constant media attention to set aside political rancor and work together to solve the entitlement funding and benefit issue. We refer to this as *NAP* (No Alternative Politics) time.

Neither party will be willing then or able to make such changes alone. Strong political leadership will see a bipartisan commission created, with required program changes debated in a civil environment. The full Congress will likely be asked to approve changes as proposed by the study group, with no ability to make modifications. Members of both major political parties will agree to avoid finger-pointing and accusations, recognizing that a cooperative effort is mandatory.

We have been at this point before and responded. We will do so again. We simply have no alternative.

Silver Bullet #3

Powerful Bond Market Pressure on the Federal Reserve to Restrain Inflation Will Ensure Low Long-Term Interest Rates

High levels of confidence in the Federal Reserve's ability to restrain inflation pressures exist today. Such confidence will continue as the nation's bond market—the Fed's overseer—will simply not allow any return of irresponsible Federal Reserve monetary policy. Such confidence will allow long-term interest rates to remain at low levels, benefiting both home buyers and others who seek funding in the credit markets.

Silver Bullet #4

Aggressive Baby Boomer Moves to Save More for Retirement Will Boost the Stock Market Sharply Higher in Coming Years

The stock market should continue to do well in coming years. More aggressive moves by Baby Boomers to build towards their retirements will provide billions of dollars of new funding monthly to the stock market. At the same time, members of Generation X, as well as older members of Generation Y, will increasingly see the wisdom in saving more aggressively for their own later-life situations, understanding that *they* are responsible for their financial futures—not government and not employers.

This powerful combination bodes well for the future of America and its people.

Index